UNRIVALED

By **Norman Jetmundsen, Jr.**
Co-Author **Karin Dupree Fecteau**

Publisher: Shakerag Hollow Press

FOREWORD

When I arrived on Sewanee's campus as a freshman, it didn't take long to hear about the famous football team of 1899. The posters about the team that played five games in six days—going undefeated against future football powerhouses before resting on the seventh day—were ubiquitous. I imagine most students had a similar experience of familiarity with the team's story. After later returning as a professor and dean, I learned more about the history of The University of the South, including the 1899 team. Yet, when my classmates David Crews and Norman Jetmundsen produced a documentary film about the team, **Unrivaled: Sewanee 1899**, I realized there was much more to the story than I had ever imagined.

Sewanee is a unique place with its 13,000-acre laboratory, playground, and sanctuary on the Cumberland Plateau in eastern Tennessee. There is an emphasis on close professor–student relationships, the Honor Code, a community founded on civility and mutual respect, and tradition. Tradition, rightly understood as learning from and retaining the best parts of the past—while being willing to change with the times and boldly anticipate the future—creates a strong bond between the past and present. For instance, Sewanee's core mission since its founding has been to focus on a broad education across many disciplines, with an eye toward educating students to think critically and holistically and to communicate clearly, within the context of a moral and ethical framework. That mission continues, even as the curriculum adjusts to meet the demands of the 21st century.

A powerful example of our tradition is the Iron Men of 1899, who accomplished the seemingly impossible and made a small college on a mountaintop proud to celebrate this amazing display of courage, tenacity, and perseverance, as well as our place in the history of college football. Sewanee's glory days as a major college football program are long gone, but its commitment to educational excellence both inside and outside the classroom, and both in the College of Arts and Sciences and our Episcopal School of Theology, remains our central focus and raison d'être. Sports are still an important part of student life, and they play a key role in forming the character of our student-athletes, who play for the love of their game: amateurs in the best sense of the word.

As we celebrate the 125th anniversary of the 1899 team, I am delighted that this book will add to the history of the team and preserve its remarkable experience for future generations. This epic story serves as a beacon from the past of what we can achieve when we work together for a common purpose: It is both inspiring and humbling, and it is a reminder that character, determination, and teamwork prevail, then and now.

Rob Pearigen
18th Vice Chancellor of The University of the South

Left: Stained glass in All Saints' Chapel commemorating the 1899 Team

4 | UNRIVALED: SEWANEE 1899

Left: The Iron Men of 1899

PRELUDE

There is and always will be spirited debate as to who is the greatest college football team of all time.

Many teams and storied programs can lay claim to that honor. One achievement, however, is beyond debate: which team had the most extraordinary single season in college football history, a season that will never be equaled, much less surpassed. To answer that question, we have to go back to the year 1899 and a small Episcopal college in Tennessee on the Cumberland Plateau, The University of the South, known colloquially as Sewanee.

Like other exceptional human endeavors, the success of the Sewanee Tigers' 1899 football season was due to a combination of vision, preparation, grit, determination, and luck in the face of numerous obstacles that threatened to derail the season.

The South was still recovering from the Civil War—which had ended 34 years earlier—and from the repercussions of defeat and reconstruction. The abolition of slavery and the Civil Rights Acts had upended the economic and social structure of the South. The University of the South, which was founded in 1858, was struggling to survive.

"The founders believed that every square inch of the 5,000 acres of land donated by the Sewanee Mining Company would be needed to create the university that they envisioned, which would be not simply colleges of different sizes but professional schools of all sorts. And they raised half a million dollars for that purpose at the time the cornerstone was dedicated in 1860." —John McCardell

This vision for Sewanee was shattered by the Civil War. Several of the University's founders had died fighting for the Confederacy, the original cornerstone was destroyed by Union forces, and the college treasury was depleted, all before a single student had matriculated to the Domain.

"The University … emerged from the war a very different kind of place from that which the founders envisioned. … There was not a penny left in the treasury. There was not a building left on the campus. And so, when they returned in 1866, there was some considerable doubt that the University would ever actually get back on its feet and open its doors." —McCardell

The University did open its doors in 1868, just barely meeting a proviso that classes must begin within 10 years or the 5,000-acre land donation from the Sewanee Mining Company would be forfeited.

Near the turn of the century, Sewanee was still in a precarious financial position. The 1899 team's extraordinary season forever cemented Sewanee's place in the history of football and gave the University a never-failing source of pride and inspiration. ∎

"There was a time, more than a century ago, when The University of the South was the baddest college football team in America." [1] —Adam Doster

DEDICATED TO:

Kelli, Jonathan, Nelson, and Taylor

"My heart is and always will be yours." —Jane Austen, *Pride and Prejudice*

Author: **Norman Jetmundsen, Jr.** | Co-Author: **Karin Dupree Fecteau**

Illustrations: **Ernie Eldridge, Jim Trusilo** | Copy Editors/Proofreaders: **Susan Alison, Taylor Jetmundsen**
Executive Assistant: **Mary Lynn Porter**

Copyright ©2024 | All Rights Reserved | ISBN #: 979-8218-42019-2 | Publisher: Shakerag Hollow Press

No part of this copyrighted work may be reproduced, republished, or used in any form or by any means—
graphic, electronic, or mechanical—without the express written permission of the author and publisher.

CONTENTS

FOREWORD
2

PRELUDE
4

A NEW GAME
8

A VIOLENT SPORT
18

FOOTBALL
AT SEWANEE
28

SEWANEE
IN 1899
38

THE 1899
SEWANEE TIGERS
44

UNSUNG HEROES
58

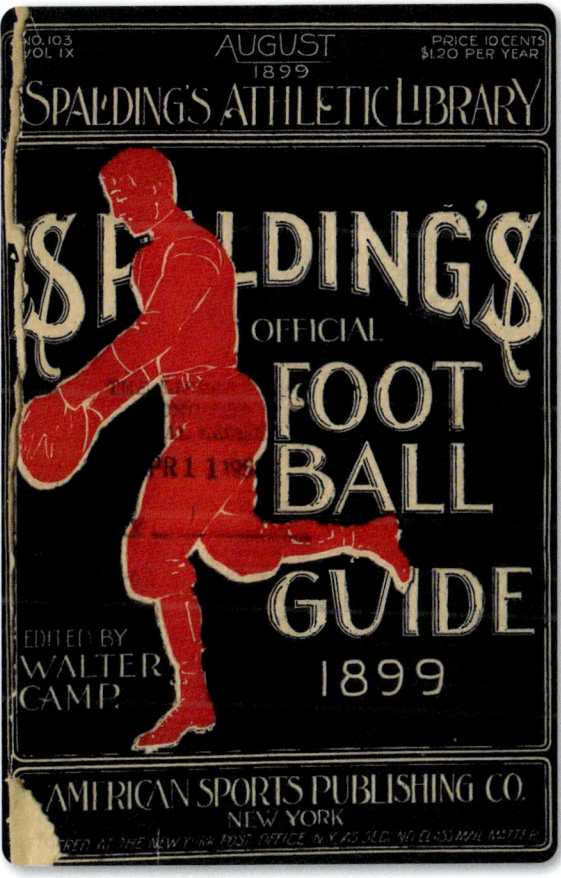

THE SEASON
64

CHAMPIONS
OF THE SOUTH
134

GLORY AND
SACRIFICE
138

SEWANEE TODAY
142

1899
REMEMBERED
150

THE
PRESIDENT'S BOX
162

THE
DOCUMENTARY
164

AFTERWORD
167

FOOTNOTES
170

CREDITS
176

Scan to listen to Bobby Horton's music score from the documentary.
©Bobby Horton

Above: SPALDING'S FOOT BALL GUIDE 1899

This page: Early football game **Right:** AMERICAN FOOTBALL, by Walter Camp, 1893

CHAPTER 1

A New Game

"Anytime anything is ever written about the history of college football, Sewanee will be mentioned." —Robert Black

In the early 1890s, the South was introduced to an increasingly popular, albeit violent, college sport called football. Football caught on in the South because it not only was exciting but also carried with it vestiges of war and manhood.

"It is no coincidence that intercollegiate athletics emerges in the midst of this discussion. This is also a time when communities, North and South, are erecting monuments to the Civil War dead. There's a whole range of activity taking place to transmit this experience of war. What comes closer to the experience of combat than football?" —McCardell

"Football became a kind of proxy experience for battlefield glory for young men who had not had the opportunity. You were supposed to fight and be willing even to die and even willing to kill for your team, for your university."
—Woody Register

"Football … was a place where young men could test their mettle: mettle of wills, of stamina, of strength, of teamwork together, not through the clash of arms but through the heat of competition on the gridiron." —Reuben Brigety

"You had the idea of muscular Christianity. You had that Victorian idea coming out of Thomas Rugby and rugby school in England. You had this sense that there was a connection between physical strength and moral virtue, a connection between physical strength and success." —Jon Meacham

The first college game was played in 1869 between Rutgers and Princeton. That game has been described by some as a "brawl."

By 1899, the game had changed and developed, although it was different from modern-day football. Teams had eleven players who played both offense and defense; however, there was no forward passing.

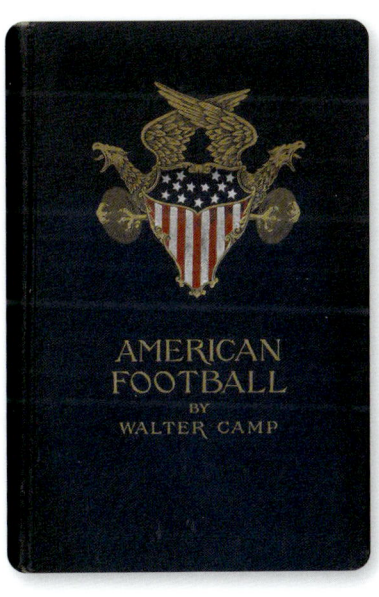

"Football at the time was really more like an English scrum rugby match. There was very little resemblance to what we call, now, football."
—Sam Williamson

"All they did was butt heads."
—Bobby Bowden

Spalding's Official Foot Ball Guide 1899 provided the rules for college football games. Players played both ways, and amazingly, if they came out of the game, they were not allowed to return to the field of play. The offense had three downs to make five yards for a first down. When the ball turned over, players who had just been on offense were suddenly on defense. The kicking game, also a critical part of the game, was both an offensive and defensive strategy. Since there was no forward passing, teams often would punt on first or second down to get the ball onto their opponent's side of the field and hope for a "muff," or fumble. The game consisted of two 35-minute halves with a 10-minute halftime.

"You didn't have huddles. Everything was sort of a continuous exhaustion game." —Williamson

"The game also moved very fast. The captain

Above: FOOTBALL CIRCA 1890 sculpture by Scott Rogers

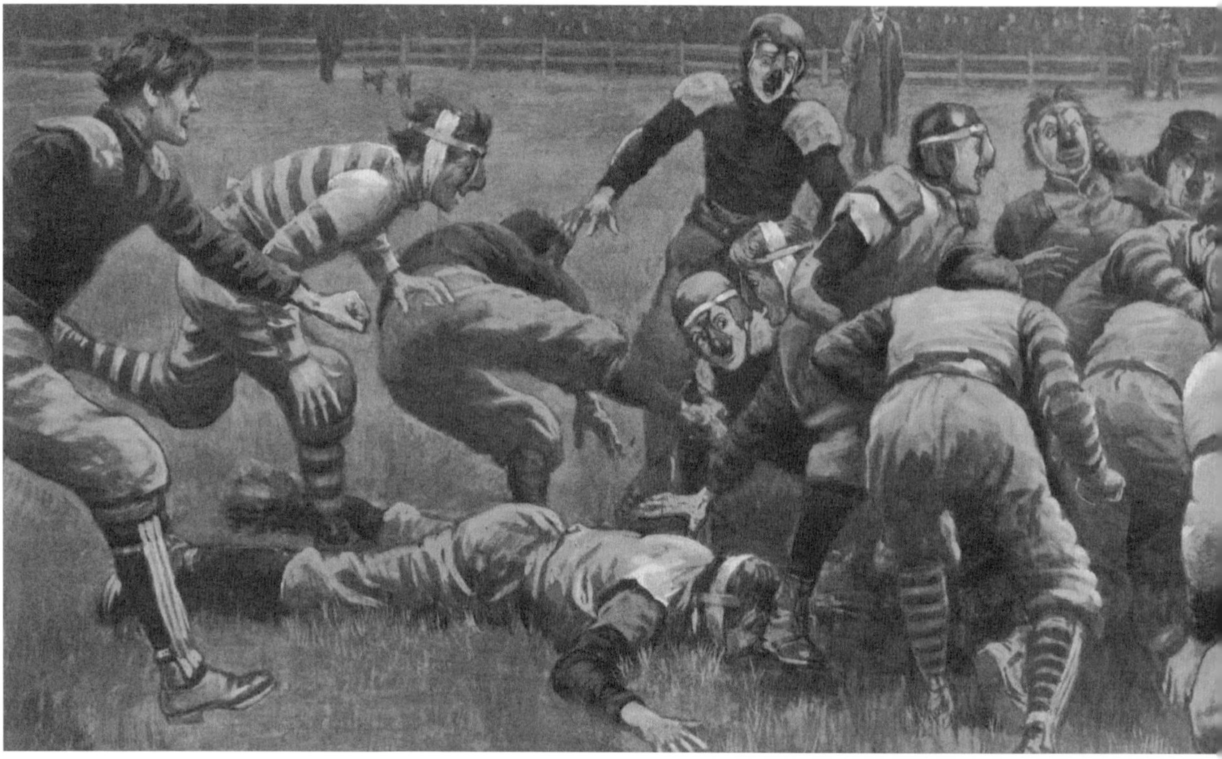

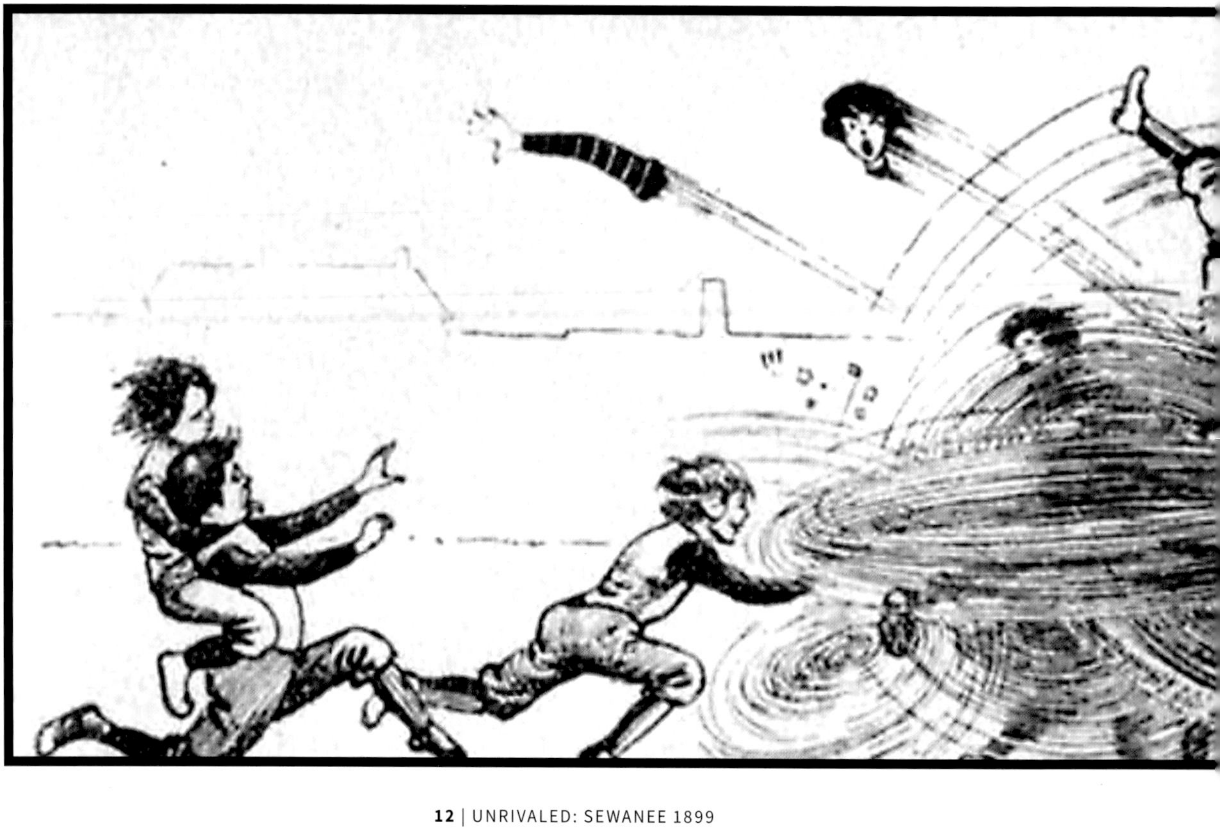

of the team would use numbered codes for plays. The minute the ball's down, you'd take formation. The code's announced, the next play. So it's boom, boom, boom, boom at a very fast pace." —Register

"They would hike the ball … and go into this whirling dervish of an offense." —Phil Savage

Scoring was different in 1899. Both touchdowns and field goals were worth five points. For a player to score a goal, he had to place the ball on the ground past the goal line, hence the term "touchdown." The point after a touchdown, worth one point, could be done with a player lying on the ground and holding the ball and another player kicking it or by a player drop-kicking the ball.

The football was much rounder and sometimes changed shapes during a game. Because there was no forward passing, it did not have to be streamlined.

John Heisman, the trophy's namesake, was the Auburn University coach in 1899. Wayne Hester, in his book on Auburn football, noted: "Heisman talked like Shakespeare to his players, perhaps because he was a Shakespearean actor in his spare time. 'What is this?' he asked, holding up a football to his first Auburn team on its first day of practice. 'A prolate spheroid—that is, an elongated sphere—in which the outer leathern casing is drawn tightly over a somewhat smaller rubber tubing. Better to have died as a small boy than to fumble this football.' " [2]

When a runner with a ball was tackled, he was considered down when either the movement of the ball stopped or the player yelled "Down!" In 1944, Ralph Black, a substitute on the 1899 team, told *The Atlanta Constitution*: "A man was never down until the ball touched the ground or he yelled 'Down.' Players seldom yelled it though because of pride." [3]

Left, top: A RUGBY FOOTBALL MATCH AS PLAYED IN THE UNITED STATES, YALE V. COLUMBIA, illustration for THE GRAPHIC, 30 March 1901. Artist is Henry Marriott Paget. [4]
Left, bottom: LIFE magazine 1903

"There were no substitutions. The players were expected, unless they were crippled or killed on the field of play, to stay in because it was unmanly—it was cowardly—to leave. They would have to drag you from the field."

—WOODY REGISTER

"There were no substitutions. The players were expected, unless they were crippled or killed on the field of play, to stay in because it was unmanly—it was cowardly—to leave. They would have to drag you from the field." —Register

"The expectation was if it wasn't a broken leg or a broken arm or something that kept you from playing, if all we're talking about is pain, if all we're talking about is blood, you were going to find a way to stay in the game and find a way to patch it up." —Tony Barnhart

"If you can get up or if you can pull yourself together, even if you're staggering—and there are accounts at the time of players staying in games even as they're stumbling and staggering around the field. You don't want to leave. You protest leaving. But, of course, players could be incapacitated, hauled off, and another comes in." —Register

Ralph Black concluded a 1950 interview with an Atlanta sportswriter by stating that "substitutions make for sissies." [5]

"I can't even fathom what the mental challenge would have been in terms of trying to play both sides of the ball with no break." —Phil Savage

The strategy of the day was known as mass momentum football. A team didn't have to have seven men on the line of scrimmage. Oftentimes, teams would take their tackles and put them in the backfield.

"It was a very rough game. There was no neutral zone. The teams could line up nose to nose against one another. The linemen were in a punching, shoving, and pushing match as they inched their way up the field." —Kent Stephens

"What mattered then was to mass force, to set bodies in motion, and then put the ball in their midst and plow forward. At the time, five of them could get a running head start, build up that momentum, put the ball carrier behind it, and then blast down like a bulldozer. The resistance against it is you go after people's legs. Elbows, knees, feet were principal weapons of attack and defense in football at the time. Use your elbow, use your knee, kick someone." —Register

The quarterback would be a quarter of the way back, the halfback would be halfway back, and the fullback was all the way back. The quarterback was not allowed to run with the ball. When he got the ball from the center, he tossed it or handed it off to one of the running backs, and then he effectively became a blocker.

One early formation was a flying wedge, where players would lock arms and create interference for the running back. Another tactic that was legal at the time was that players on offense could pick up one of their running backs and throw him over the line of scrimmage for extra yards, and players on defense could pick up one of their players and throw him over to try to break up a flying wedge.

"My father told me that in 1893 when he was a senior at the University of Alabama … they came to him and said he had to play football because they only had ten people out for football. He weighed 117 pounds. … He had straps on his uniform, and in short yardage the tackles would grab those straps and throw him over the line of scrimmage, and he would frequently, when he was telling that story, show a fairly extensive scar on his knee that he got doing that. They outlawed throwing people in 1913." —John Morrow

Coaches were not allowed on the sidelines and were not supposed to coach during the game. Scouting your opponent was also considered unethical. Therefore, the players had to be really well prepared before each game. ■

Above: "DATELINE 1905: Why Did Teddy Roosevelt want Football to be Banned?" BOOKTRIB, October 19, 2016

Above: Early football photos

17 | A NEW GAME

Above: HARPER'S WEEKLY Volume XXXV, No. 1819 (1891) **Right:** THE TWELFTH PLAYER IN EVERY FOOTBALL GAME. Part of a sensationalistic campaign against football violence in 1897, published in THE WORLD

CHAPTER 2

A Violent Sport

"It's like layer upon layer upon layer of what these guys went through that makes you just step back and really appreciate not just the grind of what they did, playing both ways, dealing with the injuries but also, oh, by the way, you could get punched, you could get bitten, you could deal with all kinds of consequences by being out there. It's just true Iron Men to be able to get through that." —Kirk Herbstreit

At the turn of the century, football was a violent sport with very little protective gear. There were around 18 or 19 deaths a year due to football, as well as many severe injuries, and there was a hue and cry to abolish the sport due to its dangerous nature.[6]

"Whereas rugby was played according to an honor code, football's code was 'Anything goes.' There were no rules against slugging, kicking, kneeing, 'face-stomping,' dirt-flinging, hair-pulling, and 'wind-milling': linemen wildly swinging their arms before the snap in anticipation of wreaking havoc. And there was biting. Sinking teeth into legs at the bottom of the pile was known as 'free lunching.' "[7]

"The injuries were going to be severe because they didn't have the protective gear that we have now. There were catastrophic injuries to the head and neck, as well as due to the rules that they had. They were vulnerable to injuries throughout the body, chest, abdomen, and lower extremity." —Robert Miller

Most players had almost no padding, and at Sewanee the matrons made their uniforms. The uniforms were usually just cotton duck pants and a jersey. Some players had flimsy leather helmets.

Herbert Smith recalled years later: "We wore very little padding with no head gear. Most of the players used a small patch of padding on their kneecap and a small patch on the hip joint. Above the waist the regular uniform consisted of a sweat shirt and a jersey."[8]

THE TWELFTH PLAYER IN EVERY FOOTBALL GAME.

"There are mouth guards and nose guards that can turn them into what looked like some kind of terrifying or frightening figures." —Register

Many players wore thick hair instead of helmets to protect their heads. Shoes were generally high-top leather boots, which had leather cleats glued or nailed together by putting strips of leather to form the cleats.

"You didn't have face masks early on, and the badge of courage of a good blocker was that his whole side of his face was always roughed up because it meant that he was sticking his face in there, a good blocker. Of course, a lot of them didn't have teeth, and that was kind of a badge of courage as well." —Vince Dooley

"Why, in my day, if you were taken out of the game you were considered yellow or that you just couldn't play well—unless, of course, you got something broken. It was quite humiliating to be taken out of a game."

—RALPH BLACK

As Ralph Black later told a reporter: "Why, in my day, if you were taken out of the game you were considered yellow or that you just couldn't play well—unless, of course, you got something broken. It was quite humiliating to be taken out of a game." [9]

"There was a lot of blood, there were a lot of teeth, there were a lot of bone fragments that were left on those fields, a lot of broken noses. It was a bit of a bloodbath especially in the trenches." —Savage

Coach Heisman was a vocal proponent of adding the forward pass and making the game safer. "Heisman campaigned for the legalization of the pass. He believed passing would make the game more exciting and less brutal. Heisman had never forgotten a day when his Oberlin team arrived at the train station after a rough game. His players were mistaken as victims of a train wreck and were offered ambulances." [10]

"My grandfather said in one of his letters that the team's motto was no body hurt, not just nobody, but **no body hurt**." —Ralph Black III ∎

Above: THE ATLANTA JOURNAL, Sunday, February 5, 1950

Above: Vintage leather helmet **Right:** Vintage football pants

23 | A VIOLENT SPORT

Left: Turn-of-the-century leather football **Above:** Morrill rubber noseguard **Below:** Leather boots with strips of leather glued and nailed together to form cleats

Right: The 1899 team motto was "No body hurt."

27 | A VIOLENT SPORT

Above: An early Tennessee game on Wait Field, Knoxville, Tennessee **Right:** 1891 Sewanee Football Team

CHAPTER 3

Football at Sewanee

"Sewanee's a fabulous combination of ecclesiastical tradition, Southern tradition, literary tradition, liquid tradition. You put all those together and it's amazing that there's anything factually based." —Jon Meacham

Sewanee began playing football in 1891. Its first game was at Hardee Field in Sewanee against Vanderbilt on November 7, and Sewanee lost 22 to 0. Since then, Sewanee has continuously played home games on what is now known as Hardee-McGee Field. It is the oldest football field in the South and the fourth oldest in the country.

Hardee Field was not, however, like modern-day grass fields. As Herbert Smith recalled: "The field this team used at Sewanee had no grass on it. It was bare mountain top ground containing much gravel, and in one corner was a large bare rock where the soil had washed off." [11]

Sewanee's second game was on November 21 in Chattanooga, and it resulted in Sewanee's first football victory when they beat Tennessee 26 to 0. This was Tennessee's first ever football game.

In 1895, Sewanee joined the newly formed Southern Intercollegiate Athletic Association, whose stated mission was for "the development and purification of college athletics throughout the South." [12] At some point in this time period, they became known as the "Tigers."

College football at the time was entirely student led. There were no athletic departments, and colleges and universities did not pay for or manage football teams. This meant that students hired the football coach, recruited players to play, and handled all the finances, equipment, and scheduling. Because these were student-run organizations without any regulatory oversight, some colleges hired what were known as "tramps" or "ringers," who were not full-time students but were paid to play for their teams. Sewanee, however, required its athletes to be full-time students.

Football quickly caught on in the South.

"There's a football mania in the Southern states that I think is unmatched in the rest of the country, and Sewanee was an early part of that. The 1890s … was the decade of football for Sewanee." —Jerry Smith

"We tend to think of football as being something that is in the blood of Southerners—Southern men, Southern women too, everyone. I'm from Alabama. I've been thinking about football since probably *in utero*. So we think of football as being something that is genetically Southern. It isn't, it has become that way." —Register

"This was a poor area of the country coming out of defeat. Anything like that, that people could do and do really, really well—they did in a coordinated way, especially, I think—probably had magnified significance for folks. Given the Scots-Irish temperament of parts of the South, if it had a little violence in it, well that was even better." —Wyatt Prunty

"You can see at the end of the Civil War how the South, because of the way they lost that war, put everything into football." —Kirk Herbstreit

"There's an absolute connection between the Civil War and the South's love of college football. There was a recovery period for the South after the Civil War, but one thing we could do is we could beat 'em in football." —Barnhart

"In the 1890s, the Civil War generation is

beginning to pass from the scene, and the participant generation is very concerned about transmitting to the successor generation, to the rising generation, some sense of the challenges they faced, of the obstacles they overcame, of the sacrifices that they've made, and how best to inculcate that in these young people, these whippersnappers, who might not otherwise have understood how tough we had it and how beneficial that experience was for us? Into that context comes the emergence of intercollegiate athletics and, in particular, of football." —McCardell

"This is 30 years before radio, clearly before movies, so you would have had theatrics, moonshine, and football . . . probably not in that order." —MEACHAM

In 1898, Sewanee went 4 and 0, but had difficulty scheduling games, in part, due to that year's yellow fever epidemic, which cut many college football seasons short. Their coach was J.G. "Lady" Jayne. Many of the players from 1898 returned in 1899, but Jayne left for North Carolina and recommended his Princeton teammate Billy Suter to be the new coach. A report in *Harper's Weekly* on the 1898 season noted: "Sewanee undoubtedly had the strongest team in the Southern Association, … but as both North Carolina and Virginia ignore the ethics of college sport and resort to illegitimate means to strengthen their elevens, Sewanee must be declared the strongest amateur college team of the South."[13] ■

Left: Football practice in Sewanee circa 1895

Everybody goes to see the games—the V. C. attends with the same regularity with which he goes to chapel, and the great and the small rub elbows along the side lines, unconscious of all official distinctions, all hearts and minds intent on that little sphere of pigskin which unites all the incongruous elements among the on-lookers into one great fraternity of eager, shouting Sewanee enthusiasts…

Above, top to bottom: 1900 CAP AND GOWN, page 177; Women attending Sewanee game circa 1900; Professors and students walking to Sewanee game in early 1900s

34 | UNRIVALED: SEWANEE 1899

Above and left: Sewanee faithful attend Sewanee vs. Vanderbilt, 1914, in Nashville, TN. "In the games in Sewanee, we know the entire community turned out, the college people, the town people, white but also African-Americans who lived in town. Now, the spectators would have been segregated. You would not have had a mingling probably of either the classes or the races, but these were events that brought the whole town together. We also know from photographs that African-American boys, unable to afford the 25-cent admission price, would climb trees or utility poles just outside the fenced-off area and watch the game." —Register

"And so a game becomes a kind of allegory for a culture striving." —Prunty (Photos: CAP AND GOWN, 1915)

TIMEOUT

Above: Sewanee vs. Vanderbilt in Nashville on Thanksgiving circa 1903/04. **Right top:** THE NASHVILLE TENNESSEAN, Tuesday, November 23, 1926

The South's First Big Rivalry

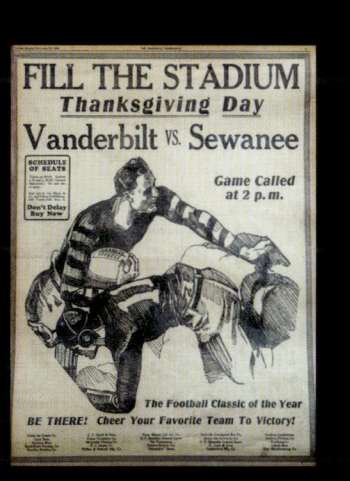

"People who cared about football in the South regarded the annual contest between Sewanee and Vanderbilt as the premier athletic event in the collegiate season. Every Thanksgiving, the Commodores and the Mountain Tigers would play in Nashville. This was a huge event. It brought many thousands of people to Nashville, and it was also Sewanee's biggest payday. Sewanee usually took home half the gate receipts, which funded its entire athletic budget . . . ." —Register

Scan QR code to listen to Bobby Horton's rendition of this song.
©Bobby Horton

Above: Music score for THE TIGER, words by B.S.M., music by T. Channing Moore, 1918. See 103-year-old Jack Blackwell's Sewanee/Vandy cheer.

Above: Breslin Tower and Walsh Hall, circa 1890 **Right:** Early Sewanee photos; the man in the buggy's front seat is Preston Brooks III.

CHAPTER 4

Sewanee in 1899

"Sewanee, like all living and growing things, has a soul and a body; and so far it has illustrated the Divine plan and has had more soul than body." Dedication, Cap and Gown, *1900 (p. 10)*

In 1899, the U.S. President was William McKinley. There were 45 states. The Spanish-American War treaty was signed that year. Horses and buggies were more prevalent than the newfangled invention called an automobile. Communication was by either slow mail service or telegraph. Electricity and lights were still novelties. Distant travel on land was mainly by train. An outbreak of yellow fever in 1898 caused, among other things, many football seasons to be cut short.

The Founders of The University of the South in 1857 had a grand vision of a large Episcopal university with undergraduate liberal arts studies, as well as schools of medicine, law, engineering, nursing, pharmacy, agriculture, and theology.

In 1866 the college was re-founded, based on the original vision but tempered by the realities of the post-war South. As the 19th century was coming to a close, the University was struggling to establish itself, and finances were always of grave concern.

By 1899, Sewanee was a small school in a town of around 1,300 people on a forested domain. At that time, the student body was all male and consisted of 326 students divided into 122 undergraduates, 26 theology students, 17 law students, and 161 medical students. The head of the University was Vice Chancellor Benjamin Lawton Wiggins. Although the football program was entirely student run, Wiggins enthusiastically supported the team.

"So on campus … things sometimes looked a little bit ragged. There were gardens around homes. There were horses. There were pigs. There were cattle roaming around town. Of course, we had dirt roads, and in the rainy season those dirt roads would be pretty wet."
—Ken Smith ∎

SOME SEWANEE RESIDENCES

SEWANEE LANDMARKS

Above: CAP AND GOWN 1900
Right: Early Sewanee photos and postcards

40 | UNRIVALED: SEWANEE 1899

St. Luke's Theological Hall, Sewanee, 1870.

Village Street, Sewanee, Tenn.

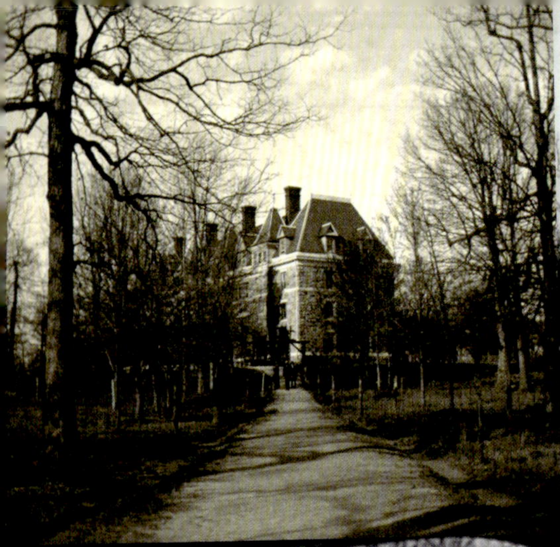
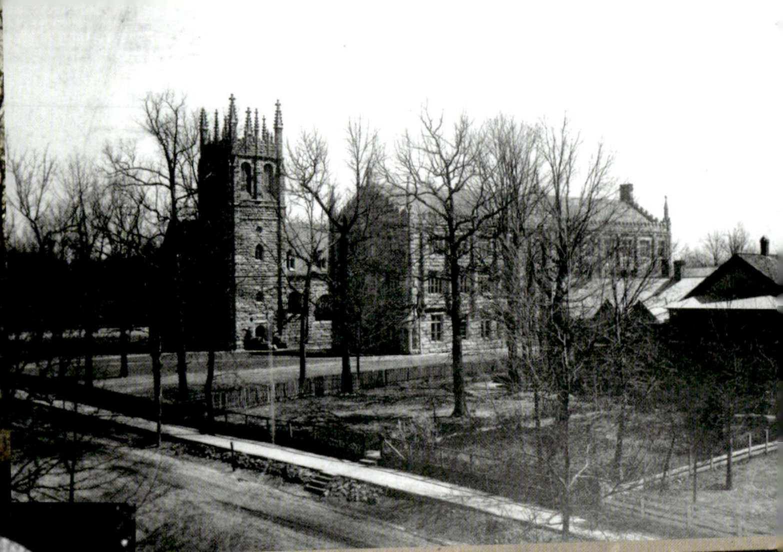
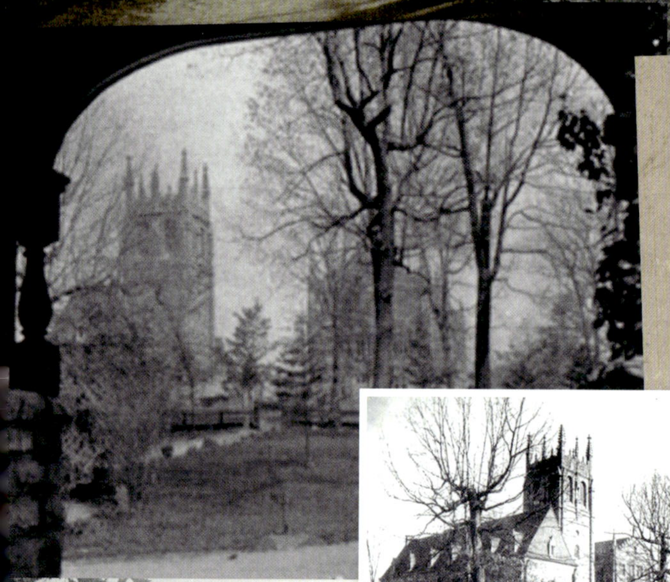
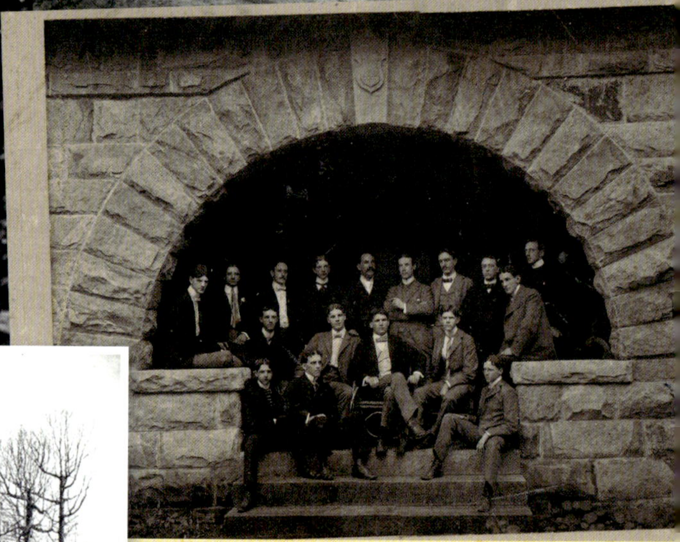
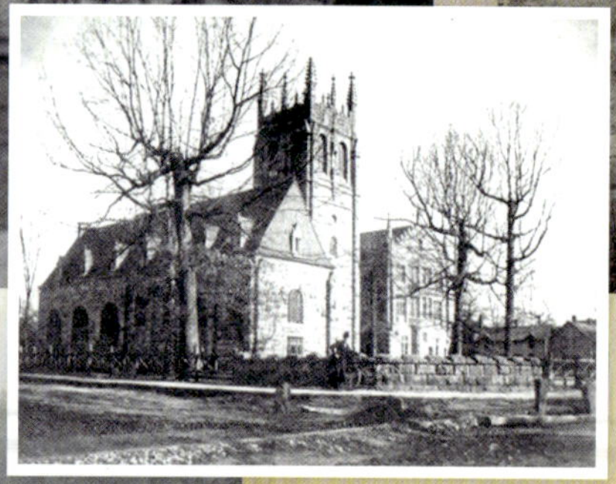
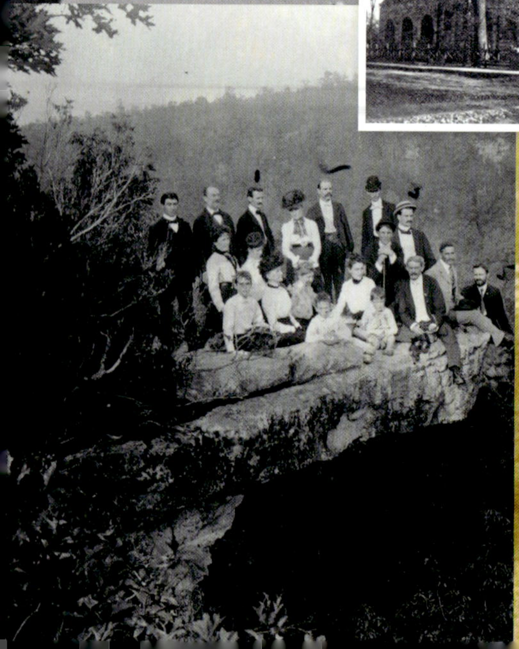
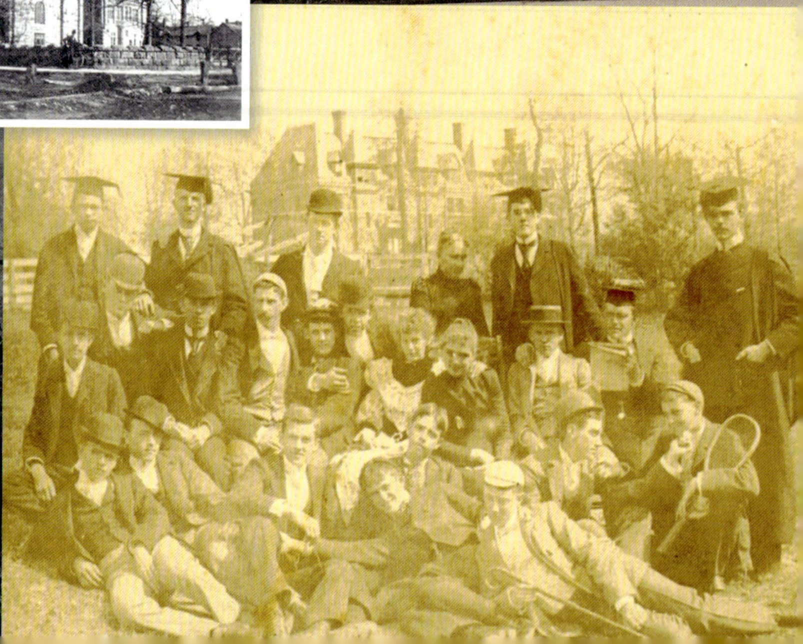

Left and this page: Early Sewanee photos, postcards, yearbook, and campus map

43 | SEWANEE IN 1899

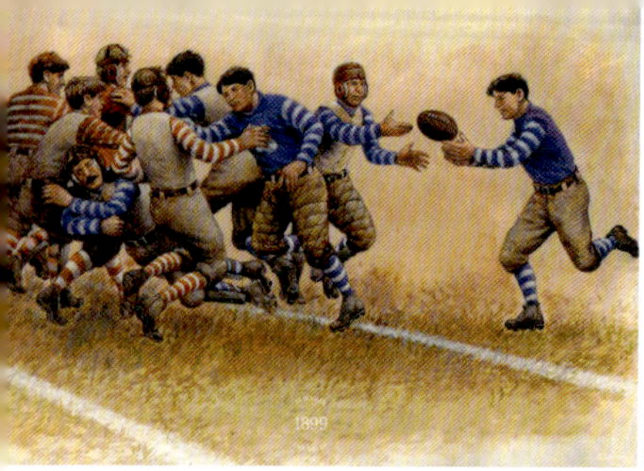
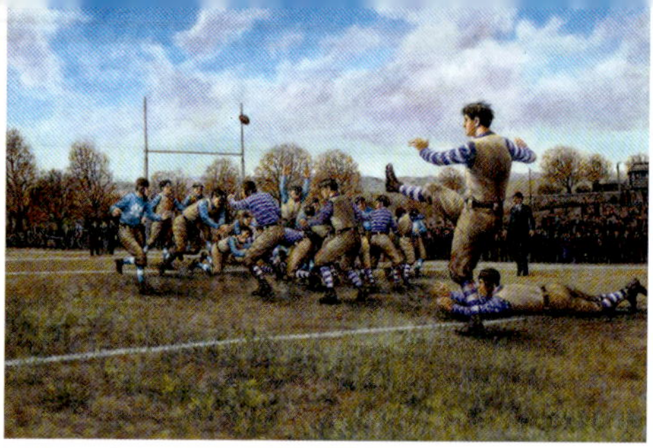
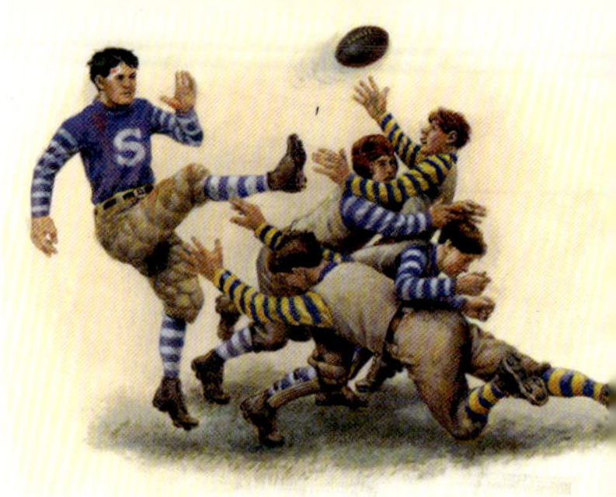
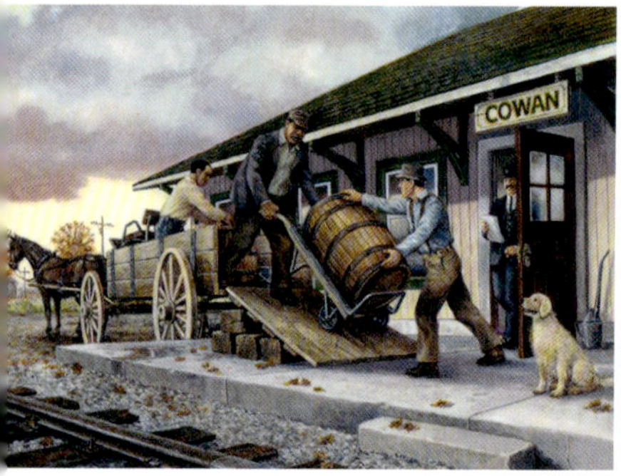
COWAN
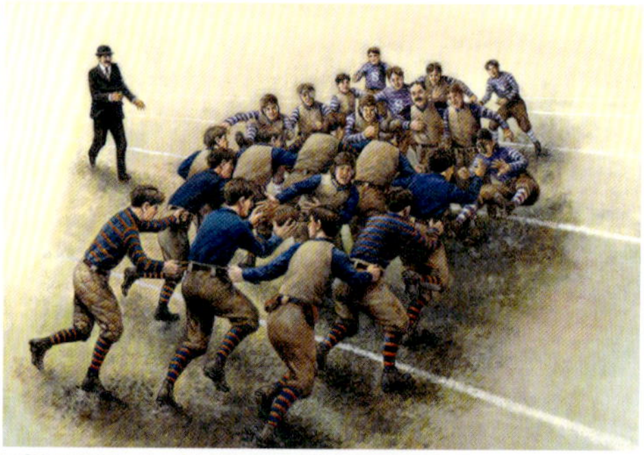
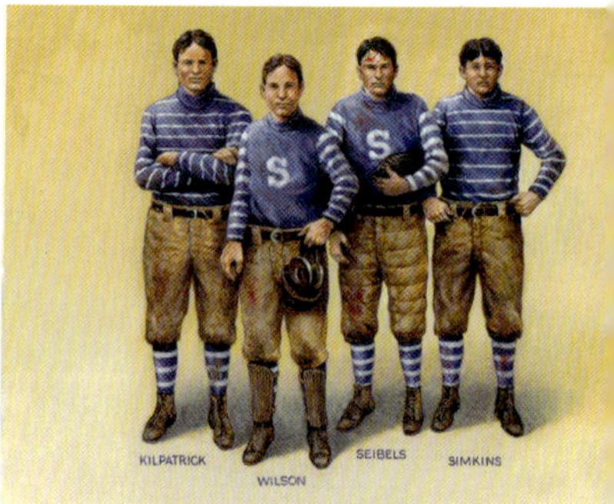
KILPATRICK
WILSON
SEIBELS
SIMKINS
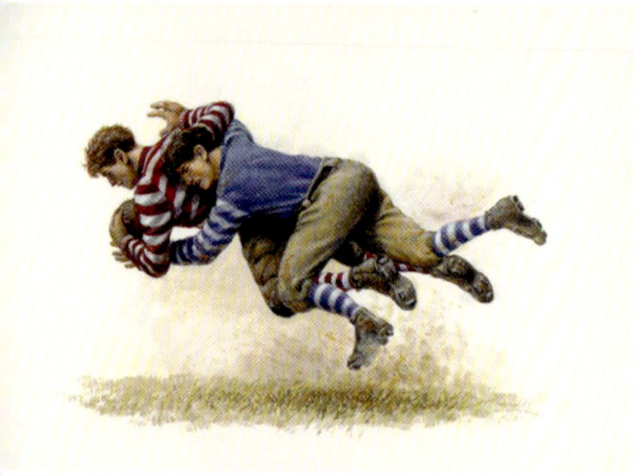
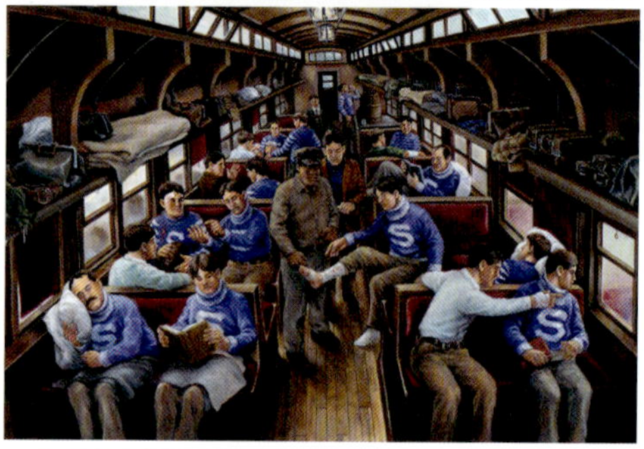
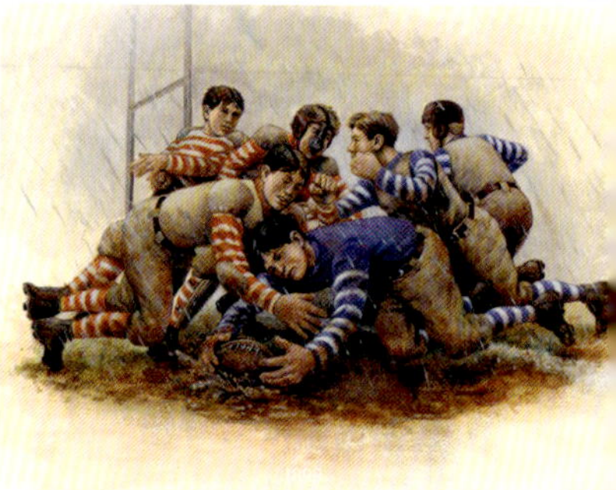
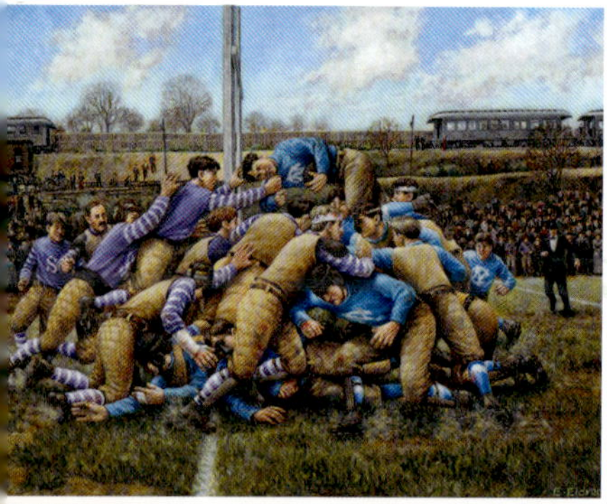
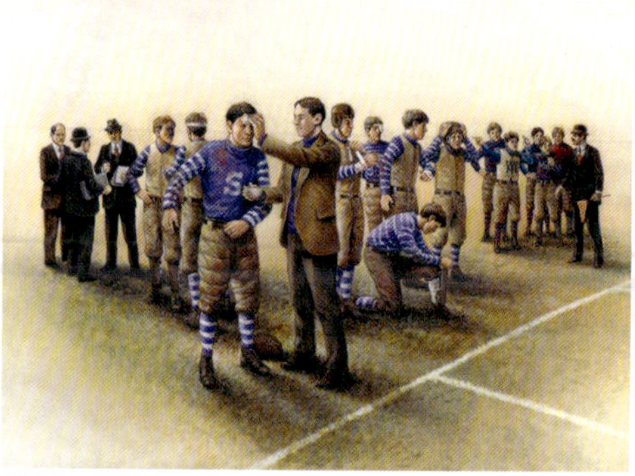
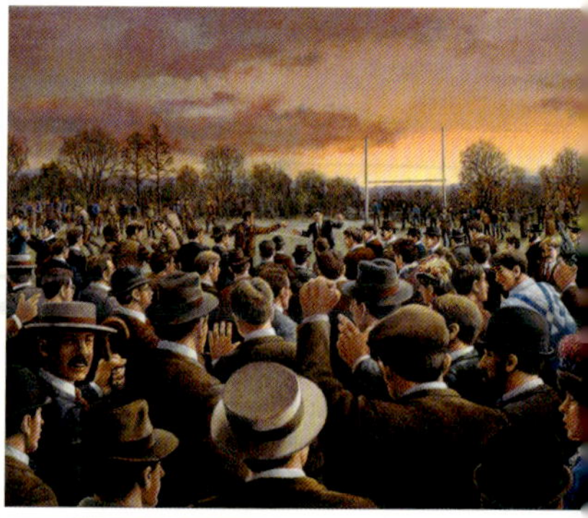
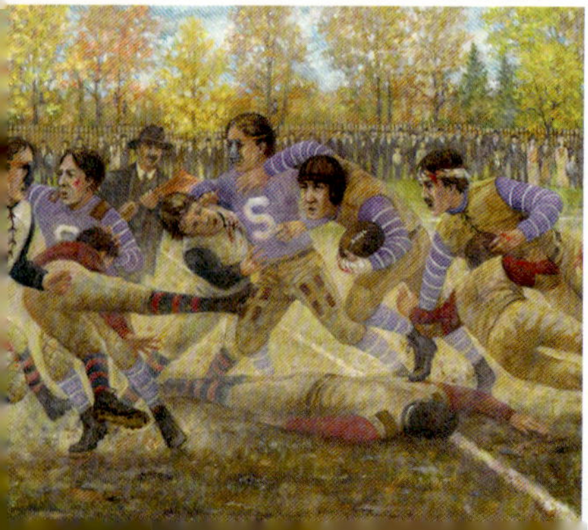
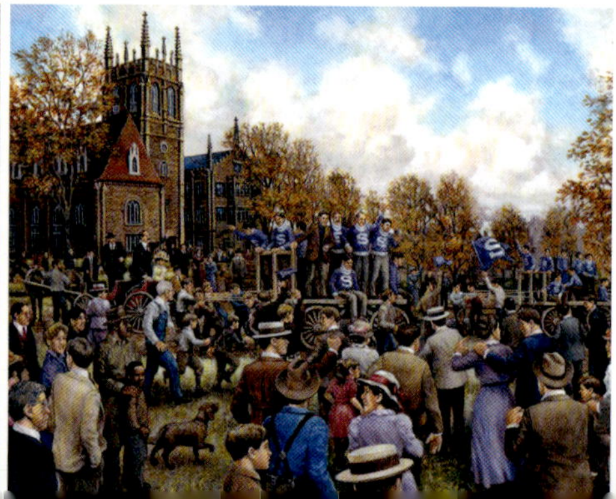
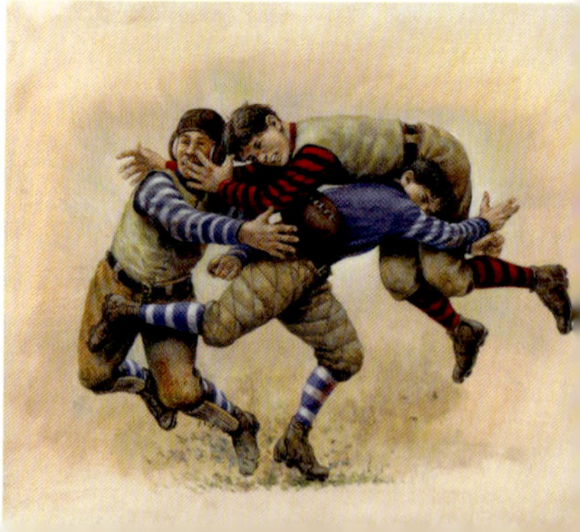

CHAPTER 5

The 1899 Sewanee Tigers

"They are probably one of the most remarkable teams in the history of college football, and everyone who cares about college football should know their story." —Woody Register

In 1899, Sewanee's football team consisted of 21 players, a new young coach, a student manager, and one or more African-American trainers. There were also several other players known as "scrubs" who practiced with the team but did not play in games. The average weight of the players was about 169 pounds. The players were all students who played for the love of the game and without any type of athletic scholarship.

When the team gathered in 1899, they had an advantage other colleges did not. Due to the climate in Sewanee, school started in the spring and went through the summer and fall. The big break was during the winter. This meant that the Sewanee football players had the summer to practice; whereas other schools did not start until the fall.

A scrub on the 1899 team, Herbert Smith, later noted that: "Speed was very important, and giving the signals while the team was lining up made the play much faster than it is today. Our aim was to run thirteen plays a minute in signal practice, and the 1899 team could do that. It took good wind to go that fast." [15]

"The players were all in the pink of condition all through the season. Practice was daily and started at 2:00 p.m. and lasted until black dark, at which time the whole squad had to run fast to the gym, some half mile away from the field. The practice was nearly all scrimmage and was very fast with little time out. Signals were called as the team lined up." [16]

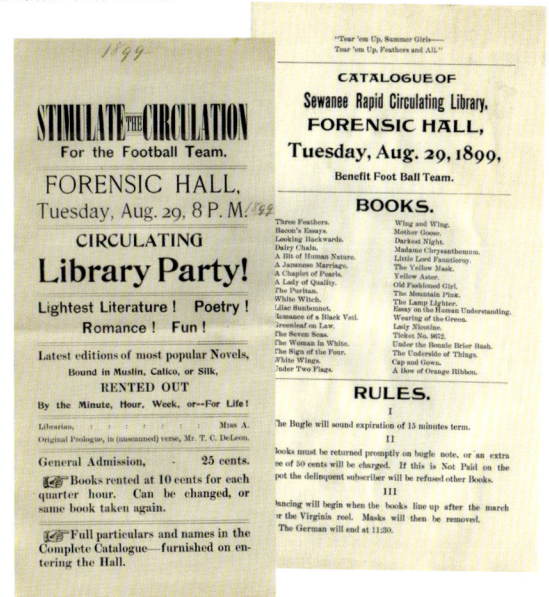

Left: Original illustrations of Sewanee's 1899 season **Above:** Fundraising for the football team

JOSEPH L. KIRBY-SMITH (TACKLE) **LUKE LEA** (MANAGER) **HARRIS G. COPE** (QUARTERBACK) **FLOY H. PARKER** (SUBSTITUTE) **WILLIAM "WILD BILL" CLAIBORNE** (GUARD) **DANIEL B. HULL** (HALFBACK)

HUGH MILLER "BUNNY" PEARCE (END) **RINGLAND "REX" KILPATRICK** (HALFBACK) **CHARLES QUINTARD "QUINT" GRAY** (HALFBACK) **BARTLETT ET ULTIMUS "THE CABOOSE" SIMS** (END) **HENRY G. "DITTY" SEIBELS** (HALFBACK & CAPTAIN)

ALBERT T. DAVIDSON (SUBSTITUTE) **ANDREW C. EVINS** (SUBSTITUTE) **WILLIAM BLACKBURN "WARBLER" WILSON** (QUARTERBACK)

(BACK) (COACH) (SCRUB)

HENRY S. KEYES
(GUARD)

WILLIAM H. POOLE
(CENTER)

RALPH P. BLACK
(END)

LUTHER GEORGE H. WILLIAMS
(SCRUB)

LANDON MASON
(SUBSTITUTE)

JOHN W. "DEACON" JONES
(TACKLE)

ORMOND SIMKINS
(FULLBACK)

RICHARD ELLIOTT "PAP" BOLLING
(TACKLE)

CHARLES BLAYNEY COLMORE
(SCRUB)

47 | THE 1899 SEWANEE TIGERS

Luke Lea

Above: Luke Lea. Ditty Seibels later wrote: "Lea was probably one of the most colorful characters Tennessee ever had." [17]
Right, top to bottom: The group that attempted to kidnap Kaiser Wilhem II, at Fort Oglethorpe in Georgia in 1919 (THE WASHINGTON POST, August 14, 2018; Photo: Tennessee State Library and Archives); Vandy coach Clark Lea (Photo: Vanderbilt University Athletic Department)

"One of the most colorful characters in the whole band of it was Luke Lea, who was a promoter—I think he was a promoter when he was still wearing diapers." —Prunty

Lea served as the student manager of the team in 1899. He had graduated from Sewanee in 1898 but came back to get a master's degree, primarily so he could run the football program. As the student manager, Lea handled the scheduling of games, hiring the coach, attending practices and games, and handling all of the equipment, finances, travel, and lodging for the team. "He was not a player. He was the athletic director because there was no such position there." —Laura Knox

When one considers that Lea, a 20-year-old student, had to arrange the 12-game schedule via telegraph and handle the logistics of train travel, lodging, food, and equipment basically by himself with no athletic staff, this achievement is all the more impressive. "Mr. Lea made absolutely every arrangement. He made the arrangements for lodging and eating, and any other logistics that had to be taken care of. He did it all." —Larry Majors

"Just think of the logistics of how he had to make it work. They had to eat. They had to sleep. They had to make sure the train was on time. They had to get to the games on time. He was the organizer and the team manager and made it happen." —Yogi Anderson

> "You'd be hiring 40 people to do that nowadays."
> —Bowden

"Luke Lea is one of the most fascinating characters I have run across in covering college football for 42 years. He's one of those people who not only has a vision but has the skillset and the determination and the persistence to pull it off." —Barnhart

"Everything he did in his life was a bit of an adventure, and I think that football team was a massive undertaking." —Crom Tidwell

"He put together a plan that just turned out to be a triumph from so many different angles." —Leah Rubino

Lea's vision and ambition are evident, in the extraordinary— indeed, some would say preposterous—schedule he crafted in 1899. These attributes were echoed later in his life, when he became the publisher of *The Tennessean* newspaper and one of the youngest men ever to be in the U.S. Senate. In a great footnote to history, he orchestrated a daring plot in the waning days of World War I to kidnap Kaiser Wilhelm II, who was exiled in Holland. His scheme came extraordinarily close to success; they actually got inside the castle before being thwarted. As Laura Knox recalled, "General Pershing was later reported to have said, 'I am a poor man, but I would've given a year's salary to have been with Lea and the boys in Holland that night.'"

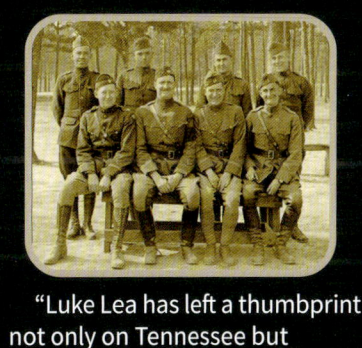

"Luke Lea has left a thumbprint not only on Tennessee but on the fiction of Tennessee. If you invented the story, you'd probably edit some of the parts out because it would seem improbable." —Meacham

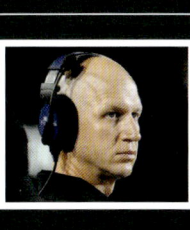

"Vanderbilt Football has been a connecting thread through my family for generations. Today, it connects my father, myself, and my three young children. As I learned about the legendary Luke Lea, it fascinated me to learn those ties go back to the 1890s. A Nashville native just like me, Luke's journey took him to Sewanee, one of Vanderbilt's biggest rivals in the South at the time. The Vandy-Sewanee game was an annual Thanksgiving tradition, excluding for one season.

In 1899, Luke was a manager for Sewanee and couldn't agree with Vanderbilt on how to split the game's proceeds; the rivalry was off. In response, that 1899 Sewanee team became the stuff of legends. They went undefeated and outscored opponents 322-10 with a grueling schedule that included five games in six days. I can't imagine doing the same today, but I know the competitive streak in the Lea family lives on." —Coach Clark Lea, head football coach, Vanderbilt University

OCTOBER

15	16	17	18
22	23 **PIEDMONT PARK — Georgia Tech**	24	25
29	30	31	1

NOVEMBER

5	6	7	8 **VARSITY ATHLETIC FIELD — Texas**
12	13 **STATE FIELD — LSU**	14 **BILLINGS PARK — Ole Miss**	15
19	20 **HARDEE FIELD — Cumberland (TN)**	21	22

DECEMBER

26	27	28	29 **RIVERSIDE PARK — Auburn**
3	4	5	6

1899

50 | UNRIVALED: SEWANEE 1899

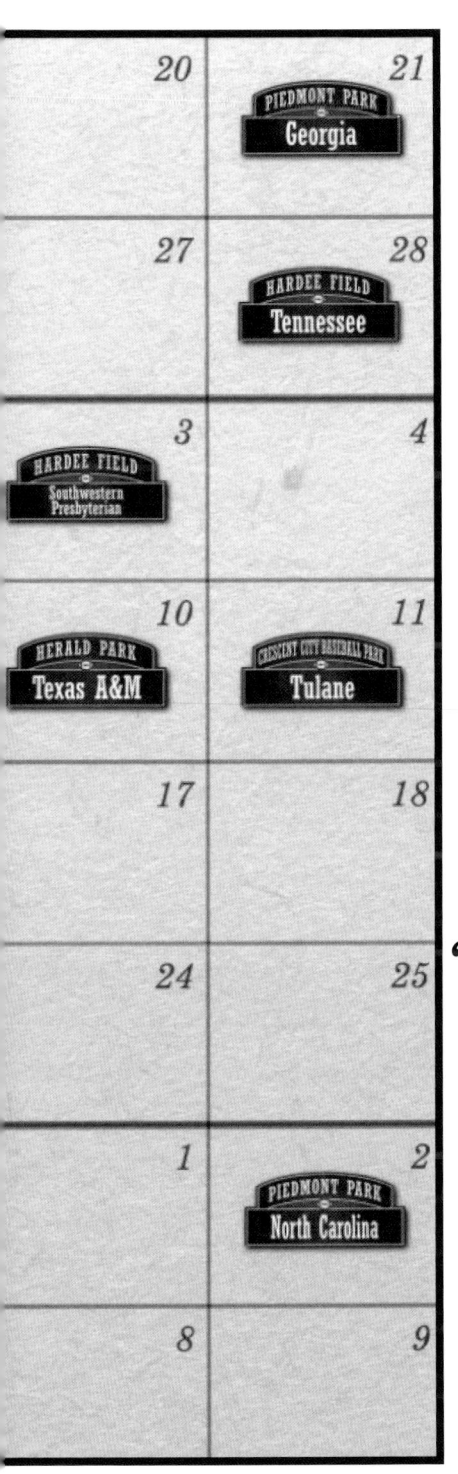

THE SCHEDULE

In 1899, Luke Lea was unable to agree on the gate-receipt split for the traditional Sewanee vs. Vanderbilt matchup, which usually funded Sewanee's entire season. In order to save the program, he had to look all over the South for teams to play to make up for this lost revenue. The result? An unrivaled season.

His efforts resulted in a grueling schedule of 12 games in a six-week period, which not only was an unprecedented number of games in the South at that time but for the first time ever required a team to travel all over the region. As part of the schedule, Lea arranged for the team to play five games in six days on the road and travel 2,500 miles by train.

"I would have loved to have been in that room when he brought up the idea. 'Hey, here's a great idea that's going to help generate some revenue. We're going to travel around the South in six days and play five games.' I mean, it's unheard of." —HERBSTREIT

Left: 1899 football schedule, art by Z-Axis **Above:** Early football game

51 | THE 1899 SEWANEE TIGERS

Sewanee was the first college team to travel such long distances to play games. Anyone looking at Sewanee's 1899 schedule, given the grueling nature of football at the time, would have concluded that this season bordered on the impossible, if not the ridiculous. Lea had set the stage for the most challenging schedule in college football history, but now it was up to the players, coach, and trainers to execute. Just who were the men that Lea thought could tackle this unprecedented and formidable schedule?

THE TEAM
Coach Herman Milton "Billy" Suter

The coach of the Sewanee team in 1899 was Herman Milton "Billy" Suter, a young man who had played football at Washington and Jefferson, Penn State, and Princeton. Suter was smart and brought a number of ideas from Princeton to Sewanee, including introducing the quick kick to the South. A substitute on the 1899 team, Dan Hull, told Arthur B. Chitty in 1954: "Herman Suter was a great man for strategy, the best I've seen then or since," and "[he] was the originator of the Quick Kick. It had never been used in the South before our team sprung it. … It was our 'secret weapon.' " [18]

According to sportswriter Grantland Rice, "Coach Suter was a natural leader … yet he was one of the strictest disciplinarians I've ever known." [19]

One man, who as a 14-year-old saw the 1899 team play, later wrote: "[S]punky little Herman Suter … . The word QUIT was not in his lexicon … ." [20]

Henry G. "Ditty" Seibels

The captain of the team that year was Henry "Ditty" Seibels from Montgomery, Alabama. [21] He played halfback and punted. His daughter-in-law, Frances Seibels, described him as follows: "Everybody called him a bulldog. I mean, what he wanted to do, he wanted to do, in business, in football, in everything. I think he just drove that team to victory by his determination. I don't think he ever thought there was anything he couldn't do."

"My grandfather was a smash player. In other words, he hit anything that was in front of him and tried to run him over. He wasn't a big man. I think he was about 5-10, but he was determined."
—Henry Seibels III

An example of his determination came in a prior season, when he scored a touchdown on a kickoff but it was called back due to a penalty. "He turned to his teammates and said, 'Don't worry. We'll just do it again.' And on the ensuing kickoff he ran it back for a touchdown."—Kelly Seibels

In 1944, Coach Suter told Grantland Rice: "I have seen few backs more elusive than Ditty Seibel [sic] … ." [22]

Ormond Simkins

The fullback of the team was Ormond Simkins. He was known as a power runner and a bruising tackler on defense. He also was a punter and field goal kicker and was considered by many of his teammates to be the best player on the team. Seibels noted that Simkins was "the best defensive player of his time and a beautiful back." [23]

Coach Suter later said, "Simkins was one of the greatest football players I ever saw, a fine kicker, a fine ball carrier, and the most terrific tackler and blocker I've ever seen. … After forty-five years I still haven't seen a better all around back than Simpkins [sic]. I have seen no one who tackled as fiercely." [24]

William "Warbler" Wilson

The quarterback was William Blackburn "Warbler" Wilson. The quarterback was not allowed to run with the ball. In those days, the quarterback received the ball from the center, handed it off or pitched it to a running back for the play, and then became a blocker.

In 1953, Wilson told a reporter that modern players gave him " 'the heebe-geebes' by going into those confound huddles all the time." [25]

"Warbler Wilson was my great-grandfather. He had gone to … the University of South Carolina and had played football there. He was studying law in his father's law office. Luke Lea, when he was putting this team together, talked him into coming to Sewanee to go to school and to play for them." —Fred Faircloth

Ringland "Rex" Kilpatrick

The other halfback was Ringland "Rex" Kilpatrick, who was known as a great runner and field goal kicker and has been called perhaps the team's most underrated player.

Clockwise from top left: Billy Suter, Ditty Seibels, Wild Bill Claiborne and Pap Bolling, and Rex Kilpatrick

53 | THE 1899 SEWANEE TIGERS

Herbert Smith later wrote that "R.F. Kilpatrick was ... one of the greatest half backs of the times in which he played and did much to earn the great name of the 1899 team." [26]

"In my opinion, you could say that Sewanee's backfield in 1899 was the South's equivalent of the Four Horsemen of the Apocalypse." —L. Majors

William "Wild Bill" Claiborne

The right guard was William "Wild Bill" Claiborne. Claiborne had a damaged eye for which he wore an eye patch during games. Claiborne was known to line up across from an opponent, lift up the eye patch, and point to his bad eye saying, "This happened to me in the last game. We'll see what happens today." He then flipped down the patch, leaving his opponent to worry.

"In the pictures of the 1899 team, if you look on the third or fourth row back, you'll see 'Wild Bill' Claiborne. He's got a pretty wild look about him."
—K. Seibels

Sewanee historian Arthur B. Chitty once wrote in a letter that Claiborne was "a rough player who didn't hesitate to employ tactics designed to frighten or distress his opponents. He had one custom of reaching across the line as the two teams were lining up and, with his left hand, pinching the opposing center as he stooped to get over the ball ... . When Claiborne was questioned as to whether he considered such tactics fair, he had a standard reply: 'Hell, this is no parlor game!' " [27]

John "Deacon" Jones

The left tackle was John W. "Deacon" Jones, who was studying theology at Sewanee and was known for his swearing ability.

Henry Keyes

The left guard was Henry Sheridan Keyes from Cambridge, Massachusetts.

William Poole

The center was William Henry Poole from Glyndon, Maryland. Seibels later wrote that "Poole was the best Center among the Southern football teams." [28]

Bartlett et Ultimus "The Caboose" Sims

Sims, the left end, was from Bryan, Texas. He sometimes kicked extra points, as well. Presumably, he was named et Ultimus by his parents to signify he would be their last child.

Richard "Pap" Bolling

The right tackle was Richard Elliott "Pap" Bolling from Edna, Texas. He played with Douglas MacArthur on an undefeated 1896 team at West Texas Military Academy. Ditty Seibels later recalled that Pap Bolling was "a tough Texan and a fierce tackler—a good defensive player." [29]

Hugh "Bunny" Pearce

The right end from Jackson, Mississippi, was Hugh Miller Thompson "Bunny" Pearce, who was about 5-feet 3-inches tall and weighed around 125 pounds. Nevertheless, years later, Coach Suter said in an interview that "Bunny Pearce ... weighed 114 pounds. He was a fine end. A hundred and eight pounds of this weight, is brains and heart. What else counts?" [30]

Above: Hugh "Bunny" Pearce **Right:** Yale vs. Princeton game in New Haven, HARPER'S WEEKLY, December 9, 1899

It was said of him: "I have seen games all over America, but never have I seen a player with the guts of Bunny Pearce—the atom who was all courage." [31]

Substitutes

One of the noteworthy substitutes on the team was **Ralph P. Black,** who was a right end behind Bunny Pearce. He played in several important games that year, and his letters and newspaper interviews in the ensuing years proved invaluable in researching the 1899 team.

Besides Black, the other substitutes that year were **Preston Brooks III, Harris Cope, Albert Davidson, Andrew Evins, Charles Quintard Gray, Dan Hull, Joseph Lee Kirby-Smith, Landon Mason,** and **Floy Parker.** One of the "scrubs" on the team that year, **Herbert Smith,** years later wrote several letters containing invaluable insights into the season that now reside in the Sewanee archives. ∎

> "This Sewanee team, I think, is a great testament and example of the culture and the attitude that that era kind of represented."
>
> —HERBSTREIT

THE FIRST LINE-UP AFTER THE KICK-OFF—PRINCETON HAS THE BALL—YALE'S FOLLOWERS IN THE GRAND-STAND ON THE RIGHT—PRINCETON'S ADMIRERS WERE ON THE LEFT.
THE GREAT YALE-PRINCETON GAME AT NEW HAVEN, WITNESSED BY FIFTEEN THOUSAND SPECTATORS.
Photographs by Hemment.

GEORGIA INSTITUTE OF TECHNOLOGY
ATLANTA, GEORGIA

Aug., 26, 1949.

to Atlanta Sept 8th Sewanee — Big Time — Dinner

Dear "Ditty";-

I dug into ancient history 1900 Annual and an old Purple; the results of which rgarding the 1899 team and Texas trip to be;

Team

H.M.T.Pearce RE	R.E.Bolling RT	W.H.Poole C
R.P.Black	J.W.Jones LT	W.B.Wilson Q
H.S.Keys LG		
H.G.Seibels RHB	R.F.Kilpatrick LHB	Ormond Simkins FB
	C.Q.Gray	B.Sims LE
	Bish.Claiborne RG	

This would make up your number of 18 players. I had believed that we had only 16 players. The following men to have made trip.

J.L.Kirby Smith — these 4 are mentioned in account of the LSU
D.B.Hull — game. I still am under the impression that
F.H.Parker — Harris Cope went along as Sub. Q. He is not
P.S.Brooks — mentioned in any of my accounts as playing,
in any of the trip games. He makes the 18th.

I met a person recently who came from Rock Hill SC., who told me about Warbler Wilson, he is OK has nice family and doing well as an Attorney etc.

Heres best regards but with the hope that we may Bend Elbows remove the Cob Webs and reminis. etc.

Sincerely,

Keith

Sewanee Athletic Association.
"DANCING SCHOOL."
ONE ADMISSION.

Scrapbook

1. **1896 West Texas Military Team, with R. Bolling and teammate Douglas MacArthur**

2. **Letter from R. Black to H. Seibels, Aug. 26, 1949**

3. **Seated: Rex Kilpatrick. Standing l-r: William Wilson, Ralph Black, and Oscar Wilder**

4. **Dancing School ticket**

5. **Football practice at Sewanee 1902**

6. **Billy Suter and Warbler Wilson**

7. **Henry Seibels**

8. **Receipt from Road Trip**

Above: Cal Burrows (Photo BEATTY SCRAPBOOK [1914] in Sewanee Archives) **Right:** W. Marichal Gentry portrays Burrows.

CHAPTER 6

Unsung Heroes

"They are there and doing that visible, but to us invisible, labor that enabled these men to be made seemingly of iron." —Woody Register

One or more individuals are not shown in the team photos, although they had as much to do with the success of the team as anyone. They were the unsung heroes who played an integral role: They acted basically as early athletic trainers and were known as rubdown men.

"The 1899 team had a rubdown man. This was an African-American by the name of Cal Burrows. And as the players had aches and pains, literally Cal would rub them down." —Kevin Jones

Burrows also acted as equipment manager by carrying the gear, doing laundry, and performing other tasks to allow the players to play.

Virtually nothing is known about him, and only one photograph of Burrows has surfaced. Sadly, the name of another African-American who helped the team has vanished from history.

"We know a lot about virtually every play that the Sewanee team executed throughout the season, but we don't know much about these rubbers except that they were there and that the players regarded their services as vital. They did the hard labor that enabled these players to be the Iron Men that they were." —Register

One reason the Sewanee players were able to play at all was these rubdown men who worked tirelessly to help the players recover from each game. After the game, the rubdown men would rub the players' legs and other bruised body parts to help them be able to play the next day. Sometimes, the pain of the players was so great that they would wake up in the middle of the night and call on the rubbers to come rub them.

As Warbler Wilson later recounted, "We had two, big, husky, colored men as rubbers, and they both were good. They rubbed those who needed it every night on the trip after the first game. ... After the game, it was impossible for me to sleep and one of these Negro rubbers would rub me, and the others in the same situation, until you went to sleep. This would often have to be repeated during the night." [32]

"The fact that there were two African-Americans who served as trainers of the team ... and neither are broadly celebrated or recognized in terms of the achievement and glory of that team is analogous to the American story as a whole ... . The fact that we're talking about it now as an integral part of this victory and an integral part of this story is a bright beacon for where we need to be going together in the years ahead." —Brigety ■

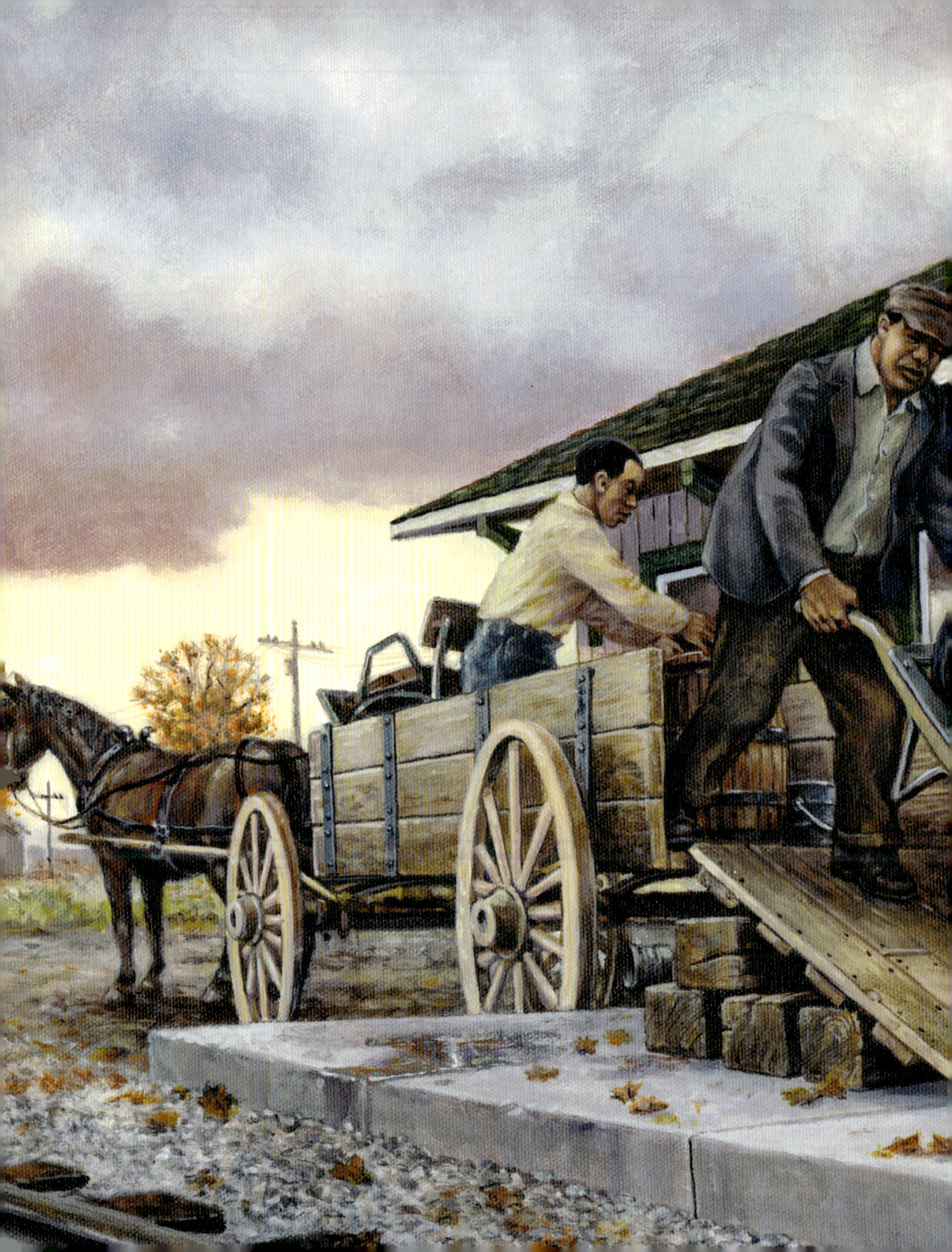

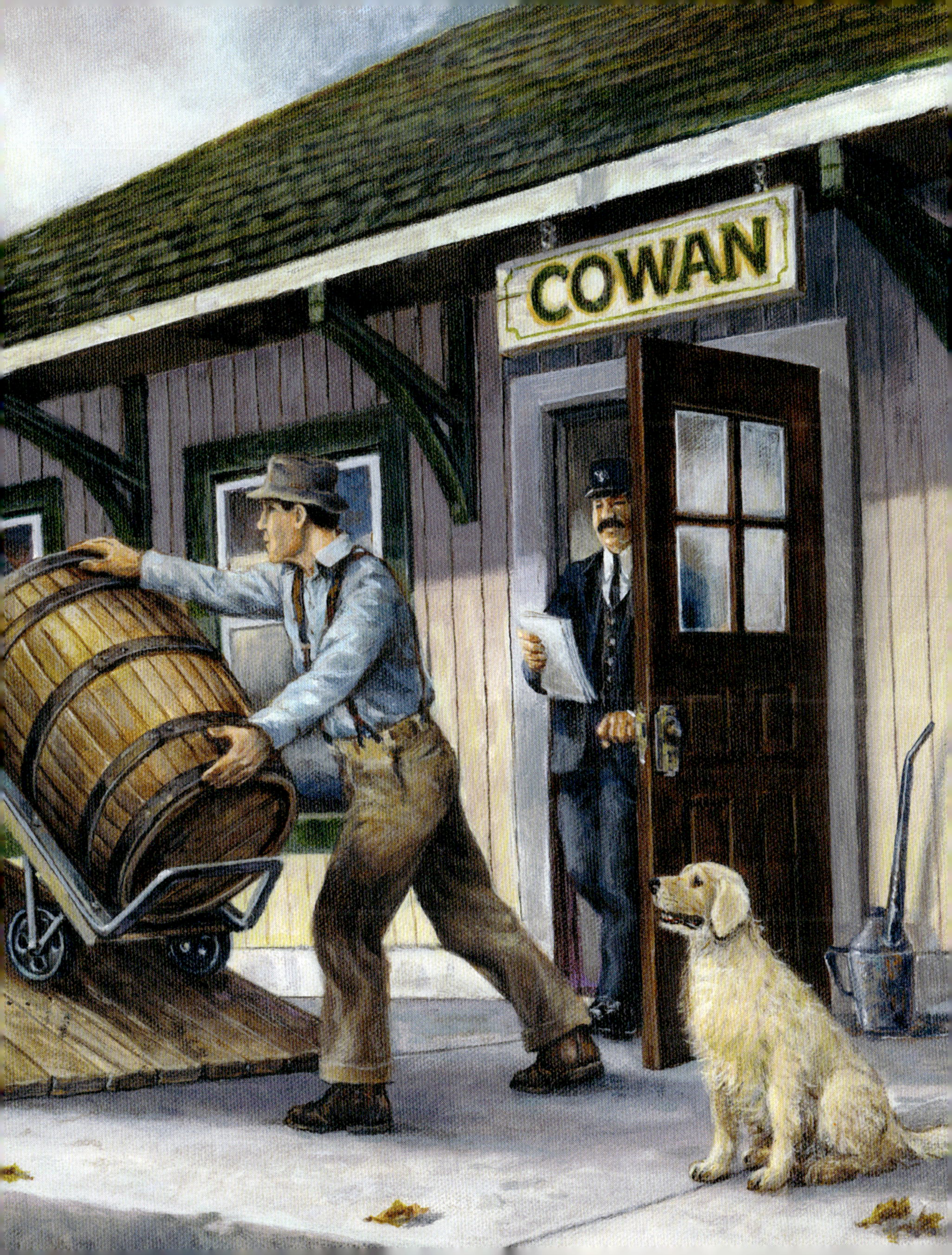
COWAN

LAW OFFICES OF
WILSON & WILSON
ROCK HILL, S. C.

October 18th, 1954.

Mr. Arthur Ben Chitty
Alumni Secretary
Sewanee, Tennessee.

Dear Sir:

Your air mail letter dated October 4th, 1954 was received by me on Monday the 11th during our term of Court in this County, and in the urgent press of other matters it was impossible for me to go into the matter until yesterday.

I looked up what few remaining pictures, etc. that I have and am mailing them to you herewith air mail as requested. I have left a few photos and paper clippings. The clipping of the team enclosed, as I recall, was taken of the men that played on the southern trip in 1899, and Coach Herman Suiter and Manager Luke Lea,- this picture was taken on the steps of old Hoffman Hall.

I don't have any snapshots taken on the t--
only one snapshot of the games played that s--
on the enclosed cardboard and shows S--
Wilson, in Atlanta against Geor--

On this -
'99 team, a--
that made
of myself
in '97 of (
Ralph Black

Yo
were not get
being a coupl
who refereed
when we beat
by General Woo
was of the Nov
demning the uni
upon me on acco
Sewanee in South
and would have g
Heisman was coach
a Sewanee team t--

LAW OFFICES OF
WILSON & WILSON
ROCK HILL, S. C.

-2-

The Alabama substitutes were placed along the side lines and kept coming into the interference. We were playing outside the City limits, no police protection and the large **crowd kept closing** in when the game was stopped by Woods because the teams didn't have a 100 feet square space to play in.

Ditty Seibles had a special acquaintance on the Alabama team and he had a big gash over his eyebrow and was flopping down and bled profusely. If it is possible for you to get a copy of the article of General Woods from the old files of the newspaper, I would greatly appreciate a copy thereof. (The above remarks are off the record for we as a team never complained about the matter and could and would have taken care of ourselves.)

In regard to what happened on the trip; I don't recall any unusual incidents. I don't know if any of us thought about or if anything was said about we might be making American Sports History. We all realized we were up against the best teams in the south and that it would be a tough schedule, but I never saw or ran into any indication that all of us didn't have any thought but that we could and would win. Eddie Miles was looked upon as our trainer under Suiter's direction.

There are no little storeis about team members being rubbed on the train between games. This was regular routine. We had two, big, husky, colored men as rubbers, and they both were good. They rubbed those who needed it every night on the trip after the first game. On Sunday in New Orleans a number of us spent a big part of the day in the hot baths in the gymnasium. Under our system of play the quarter-back had to lead the interference on out-side tackles and end runs. In every game on the trip, beginning at Austin, they would put two inch rubber bandages on each of my legs beginning on the foot below the ankle, up to above my knees. This, in my opinion, took care of the situation to a great extent, but after the game it was impossible for me to sleep and one of these negro rubbers would rub me, and the others in the same situation, until you went to sleep. This would often have to be repeated during the night. The general atmosphere was not serious, frivilous or hilarious.

In regard to the question of the feelings of the team toward Luke Lea, who made the merciless schedule. I never heard any --ll or saw any feeling at all about it being merciless. I -- the team that did not have the highest regard --nd certainly did everything in his power t-- during his entire

LAW OFFICES OF
WILSON & WILSON
ROCK HILL, S. C.

-3-

can remember a number of things in regard to different
what you call outstanding incidents. The team as a
s in the game. The turning points of each game was main-
at extent the way the team had been coached to play, and
game and not let up.

the Sewanee-North Carolina game in Atlanta on Monday,
ust following the Sewanee-Albany game at Montgomery on
was won by the hard, continued playing of the whole
In the first half within five yards of Sewanee's goal,
bucked the line eight times. There were two or three
which gave them half the distance of the goal and a first
was within two or three inches of the goal, but on the
y were thrown back several yards and Sewanee kicked the
econd half of this game, I was playing the back-field,
, and North Carolina kicked, it was a high spiral. I
fair catch on the 42 yard line and was tackled, which
yards and the choice of play. We were about ten yards
line, I called Kilpatrick and held the place kick,
x or eight feet above the cross bars for the five points
the final score in the game.

Very truly yours,

Left: Letter from Wilson to Arthur Ben Chitty, October 18, 1954
Above: William "Warbler" Wilson

Pages 60-61: CAL BURROWS MOVING TREMLETT SPRINGS BARRELS

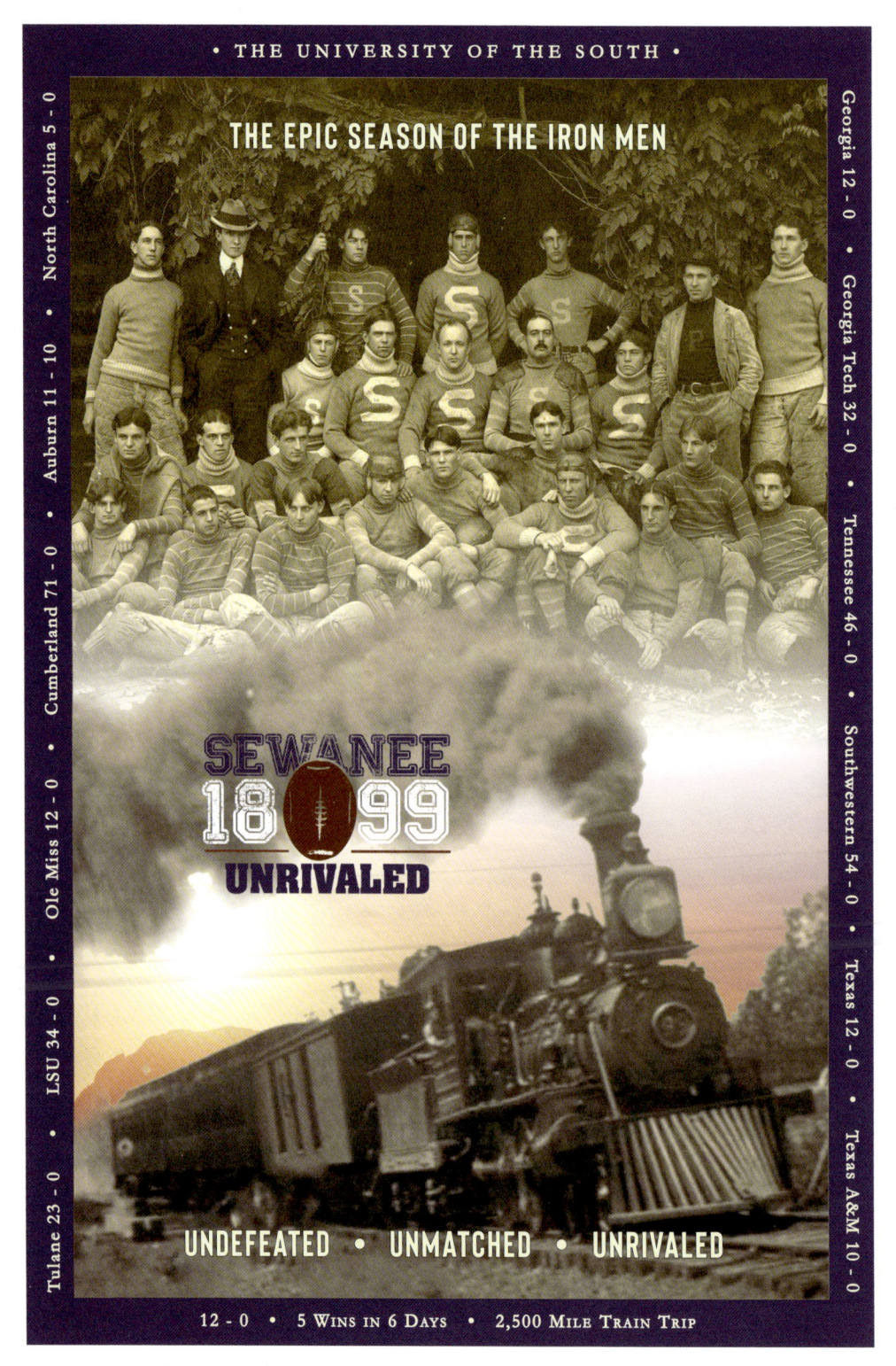

Above: Poster for UNRIVALED documentary film **Right:** Sewanee practice 1900

CHAPTER 7

The Season

"These were young men who did something truly extraordinary. They had done something that no one else had ever dreamed of doing and that no one else would ever do. They hoped to win a championship. They ended up going down in history—and they did it for the love of the game." —Woody Register

By the time the season started, the Sewanee players had been practicing for many months.

This paid off in the conditioning and teamwork of the 1899 team. Years later, Ditty Seibels wrote: "Perfect teamwork and constant study of plays and tactics enabled this team to perform its miraculous feats." [33]

Conditioning was critical for football players at the time because it was a very fast game. There were no huddles, and as soon as one play was over, the offense lined up and the quarterback or captain called numbered codes for the next play, and they ran it. Basically, football was a continuing, exhausting, hurry-up, no-huddle offense. There were also many punts during games and, of course, players had to play both sides of the ball without an opportunity to take a break during the game. This also meant that players were not particularly heavy, as the lighter, faster players were more effective and could make it through an entire game.

Georgia

SATURDAY, OCTOBER 21
Piedmont Park
Atlanta, Georgia

Sewanee began its season on the road in Atlanta against Georgia. Sewanee won the game 12 to 0. [34]

GRAND STAND
...SEWANEE-GEORGIA GAME...
25 CENTS.

GAME 1

THE RED AND BLACK.

Vol. VII.　　University of Georgia, Athens, Ga., November 4, 1899.　　No. 1.

Georgia 10, Clemson 0.

In the mud and slush of an ideal Athens day Georgia again gave to Clemson College a defeat that made their spirits truly damp. This was the first game of the season here, and on account of the rain, which came in torrents all during the game, little could be judged of what our team would do in the future. The students and a good number of town supporters came out to see the game.

The 'Varsity secured one touchdown in the first half and one in the second by hard line bucking. Hall's playing being a feature of the game. The Clemson team proved to be a very clever crowd of men, and we hope to meet them again in the future, when we trust it will be our good fortune to give them better treatment in the shape of weather.

Sewanee 12, Georgia 0.

The defeat of our team at the hands of Sewanee in Atlanta on Oct. 21 came somewhat in the nature of a surprise to the supporters of the Red and Black. None expected that the outcome would be such a decisive victory for our opponents, and many thought that Georgia would win.

During the progress of the game the weaknesses of our team were clearly shown. As regards material we proved ourselves the equal of Sewanee if not her superior. Her superb team work was gained by a long training the benefit of which Georgia has not had; her coach having been with her for but a little of two weeks prior to the game.

However it cannot be denied that if Georgia had played the game the should have done, the score would have been different, and the outcome doubtful. The game was lost through carelessness, and not through the lack of good material and efficient coaching. Saussy did his best and if the team had followed his directions there would have been many more happier beings in Athens than there were.

downs against the "smiths." As was the case with the other two games G— playing was g— not yet devel— work. Shan— McIntosh, a made fine run and quarter usual, showe— ties for his p— kicking for Four touch d— the first half on account o— and better p— of the visiti— held down to

The Techs players got i— dash and de— the very las— they have th— scoring. T— were unable— whenever t— either a kic— back, it al— for Georgia successful i—

TECHS.		GEORGIA
Cunningham,	center.	Watkins.
Hudson,	r. g.	Gol.
Griffeth,	l. g.	Lindsey.
Holman,	r. t.	Ritchie, Capt.
Woolley, Capt.	l. t.	Hamilton.
	r. e.	McCutcheon.
Neal,	l. e.	Shannon.
Dean,	quarter.	Young.
Manly,	r. h.	McIntosh.
Sullivan,	l. h.	Simcox.
Clarke,	full.	Hall.
Maddox,		

The Techs kicked off, their fullback making a complete failure by digging his toe deep into the broken ground and raising a cloud of dust, while the spheroid went hardly the required distance. Shannon, Johns, Simcox, Richie and McIntosh made repeated gains around both ends and occasionally through guards and tackles, until Shannon landed the first touch-down in seven and a half minutes.

Within three minutes Georgia scored again, the principal features being the long end runs of Shannon, Simcox and McIntosh, and five line bucks by Hall. The next three scores were made in the same manner, in three and a half minutes and two and a half

Ga.-N. C. Debate.

and no matter which side falls to Ga., she will have room to spread herself, and she must do it.

In a few days it will be known which side we are to uphold. The preliminary contest for selecting our two representatives will occur on the first Saturday after Xmas, giving the candidates the benefit of the holiday vacation for full and thorough preparation.

It is to be hoped that the students will not be shy about entering this contest. Let every one who can speak try for a place, and from this number two representatives may be chosen worthy of the greatest trust of Georgia's greatest institution.

It is a matter of regret that our law students are debarred from this contest, yet we have good material in the academic department which, with proper application, can win out for Ga. Let us get to work. A victory in forensic contest over the "Tarheels" would retrieve some of the disasters of last year.

gained little by it— They held the Georgia boys down pretty well, allowing them to cross the

Prof. R. E. Park.

Prof. R. E. Park Jr., of La— next Pr— rsuant to d of Trus— eting in h has been y for the the begin— he sent in e effect on applicants of which as chosen. ute to his d a teach— vay merits has been ducational some years red an en— his erudi— d his abili—

also be a d— the social y, and THE ends a cor—

While we rejoice that Prof. Park will be with us, we greatly deplore the loss of Dr. Riley who by years of consistent and conscientious work has endeared himself to all. THE RED AND BLACK voices the sentiment of the University when it wishes for this estimable gentleman a most prosperous career in whatever field he may choose.

Thalians.

The Thalians will shortly reorganize and receive applications for new men. There seems to be an abundance of good material in college this year, and a great performance is looked forward to. Although it has not been decided as yet what sort of play will be given, it is generally understood that the Thalians will not vary from their old habit of giving an hour of minstrel performance. The practices will be begun for this immediately after the foot ball season closes.

Mandolin-Guitar Club.

The Mandolin-Guitar Club organized last week with a membership of ten. Frank Happ was elected president and lead—

Left: Georgia team 1899 **Above:** This photograph of Ormond Simkins kicking a field goal after he scored a touchdown is one of only two photographs of a Sewanee game in 1899. Note the player lying on the ground who would have been holding the ball for Simkins to kick.

Above: FUMBLE! Sewanee vs. Georgia

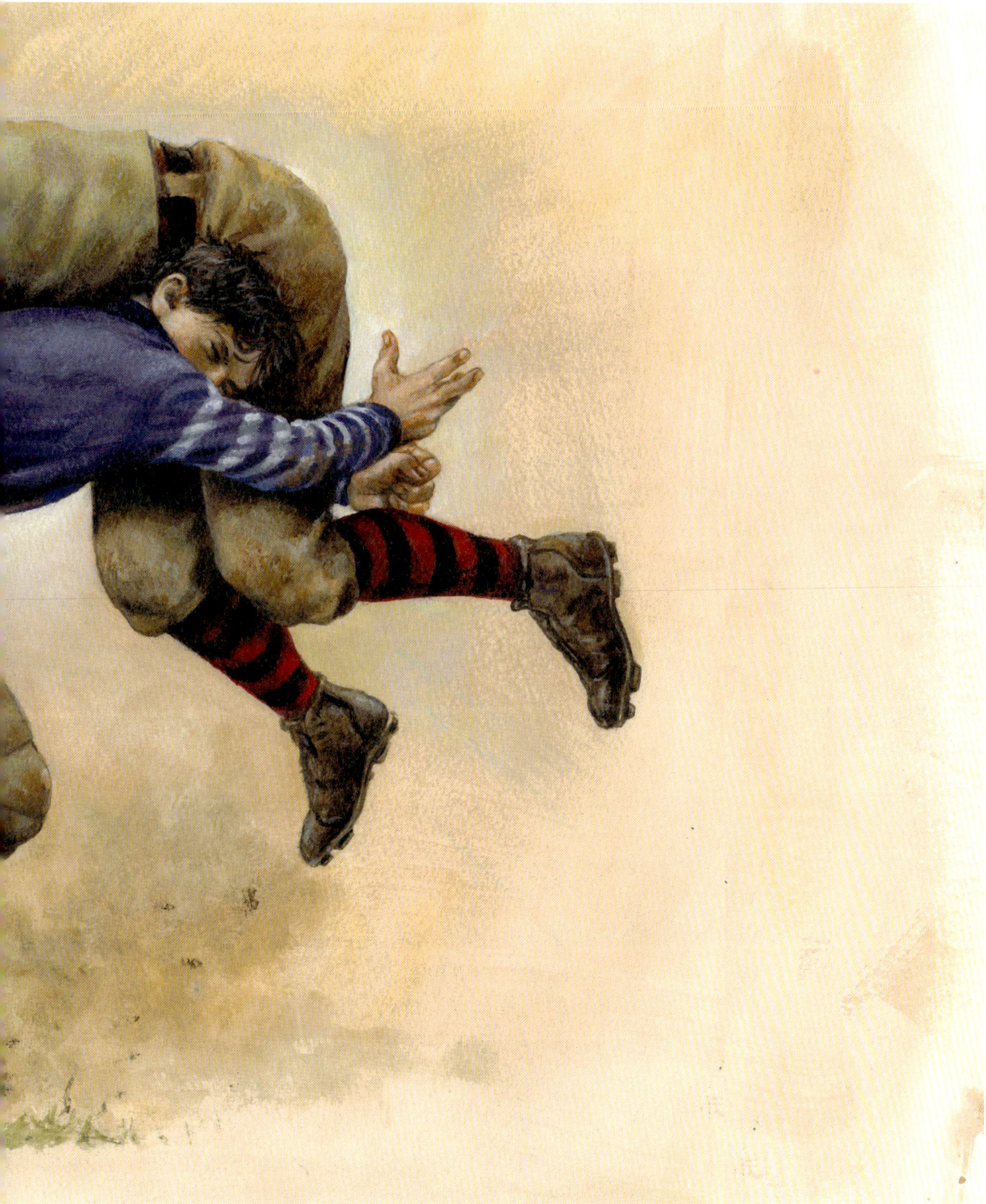

Georgia Tech

MONDAY, OCTOBER 23
Piedmont Park
Atlanta, Georgia

On Monday, October 23, also in Atlanta, Sewanee handled Georgia Tech 32 to 0. During that game, Ditty Seibels scored four of the team's six touchdowns, despite having had one long 75-yard scoring run called back due to a penalty.

GAME 2

Above: Georgia Tech team 1899

THE CONSTITUTION

SEWANEE IS V[ICTOR]

Tech Eleven Was Def[eated]
Boys Yes[terday]

SCORE, THIRTY-[TWO]

An End Tackle Pl[ay]
Proves Ser[viceable]

SEIBLES MADE SE[VERAL]

One Time for Eigh[ty]
Boys Were Ou[t]
nee's Interfe[rence]

Sewanee won, of c[ourse]
was only 32 to 0, wh[ich]
of the good work d[one]
Maddox, should enco[urage]
to work harder.

Sewanee's mass pla[y]
end, was the sensat[ion]
won them long ga[ins]
every time it was t[ried]
runs of eighty, sixty
with this play, whi[ch]
unable to stop in [time]
full back tackles, a[nd]
efforts.

The Atlanta Constitution
Oct 23, 1899

SEWANEE WILL PLAY TECHS TODAY

Teams Will Contest on Gridiron at Piedmont Park.

GAME WILL BE HARD FOUGHT

Techs Are Stronger Than They Were Last Week.

THEY HAVE BEEN PRACTICING HARD

Referee Will Have Game Begun at 3 Sharp—Pass Checks Will Be Given at Fair Gates.

Piedmont park will be the scene of an interesting football contest this afternoon at 3 o'clock, the teams of the Georgia School of Technology and the University of the South meeting in a fight for supremacy.

ATLANTA, GA., TUESDAY OCTOBER 24 1899

[EA]M
[VIC]TORIOUS

[defeat]ed by Tennessee
[Satur]day.

[T]WO TO NONE

of Sewanee's
[Sensa]tional.

[SEVER]AL LONG RUNS

[Forty] Yards—Georgia
[Outcl]assed—Sewa-
[nee Interfere]nce Good.

[cour]se, but the score
[whic]h fact, with that
[made] by Sullivan a[nd]
[ena]ge the Tech boys

[in] skirting the right
[run] of the day, and
[two] and touchdowns
[score]d. Seibles made
[and] thirty-five yards
[and] the Techs seemed
[an]y way, except by
[that] Merritt made poor

This time there is only thirty-seven yards between him and the goal line. So his run behind the same excellent interference is limited to that number of yards. He gets a touchdown. Simkins kicks a goal, and the score is 22 to 0, with seventeen minutes of play consumed.

It now takes Sewanee only one and one-half minutes to cross the goal line again. One exchange of kicks and a fumble gives Sewanee the ball forty yards from the Techs' line. This time Seibles makes the distance around the same right tackle and end behind the same interference. Simkins fails to kick the goal, and the score is only 27 to 0.

At this juncture of the game the Techs fail to take advantage of their only opportunity to score, and have a goose egg chalked against them in consequence. Merritt kicks to the forty-five-yard line, and Pearce gets ten yards before he is stopped. Simkins then drops back to kick, but before he can do so the ball is blocked by Woolley, who is hit hard by it. The ball rolls to Sewanee's ten-yard line, but a purple man is on top of it.

Seibles makes another one of his brilliant runs. This time he is tackled, after making sixty yards, by Merritt. Time is up and the first half is over, with a score of 27 to 0.

Techs Play Better.

Maddox takes the place of Merritt in the second half, strengthening the team wonderfully. Neal is put at right end and Hudson at guard. Galleher takes Gray's place at half.

During the entire half the Techs play much better than in the first part of the game. Maddox always tackles well, and Seibles did not pass him one time. Other members of the team also braced up and played with some more spirit. But the quarterback showed bad judgment in his choice of plays. He lost several yards on a fake pass and a crisscross, but he would call for it again.

Tennessee

SATURDAY, OCTOBER 28
Hardee Field
Sewanee, Tennessee

The following Saturday, October 28, Sewanee hosted Tennessee at home and was victorious 46 to 0. A scrub on the team witnessed the Tennessee game and noted: "The Tennessee game was played in a heavy rain. One play ended in a puddle, and a Sewanee tackle's head was forced under the water. His legs were free, and he did a lot of kicking before the players got off of him. He spit mud for a day or two." [35]

A special student yearbook on athletics observed: "Until the referee's whistle sounded the end of the game, the crowd stood in the drenching rain and cheered itself hoarse." [36]

GAME

3

Left, top to bottom: Tennessee team 1899; SEWANEE ATHLETIC SOUVENIR, 1901 **Above:** TOUCHDOWN! Sewanee vs. Tennessee

GAME 4

Southwestern Presbyterian

FRIDAY, NOVEMBER 3
Hardee Field
Sewanee, Tennessee

Sewanee remained at home to play Southwestern Presbyterian, now known as Rhodes College. This was their very first game of what is now one of the oldest rivalries in the South. The game resulted in a resounding Sewanee victory 54 to 0.

FOOTBALL NUMBER
The Sewanee Purple
UNIVERSITY OF THE SOUTH, DECEMBER 14, 1899.

THE SOUTHWESTERN PRESBYTERIAN UNIVERSITY GAME.

On Friday, November 3, Sewanee defeated the S. W. P. U. team by a score of 54 to 0. Sewanee continued her strong game as shown the week before against Tennessee, and the visitors were utterly unable to cope with our team. Sewanee followed up former tactics in kicking and running with the ball, and in a short game were able to run up a very large score. The backs, as usual, did most of the ground gaining, and in their fierce line plunging were greatly helped by the steady work of the line men. The game lasted thirty-two minutes, having been called early in the second half owing to injuries to the Clarksville men.

Top: THREE YARDS AND A CLOUD OF DUST, Sewanee vs. Southwestern Presbyterian **Right:** Southwestern Presbyterian team 1899

74 | UNRIVALED: SEWANEE 1899

FOOTBALL SQUAD.

75 | THE SEASON

Train Travel

For many years, the train from Sewanee to Cowan was affectionately referred to as the Mountain Goat.

It earned its name due to the steep climb onto the Cumberland Plateau from Cowan, which at the time was the steepest slope in the world for a railroad line. In Cowan, passengers would change trains to travel to their final destination.

"Sewanee was located in the middle of nowhere. The team, to play anybody, had to get on a train and ride." —Williamson

"Because of its kind of remote, mountainous location, it wasn't an easy place to get to. It was very difficult for teams to travel there. Being a very small community, there was not much of a guarantee for a team to come play there. In the first decade or more of Sewanee's football history, they played maybe two-thirds of their games away from home." —Stephens

Left: Sewanee Depot **Above:** Various Mountain Goat trains

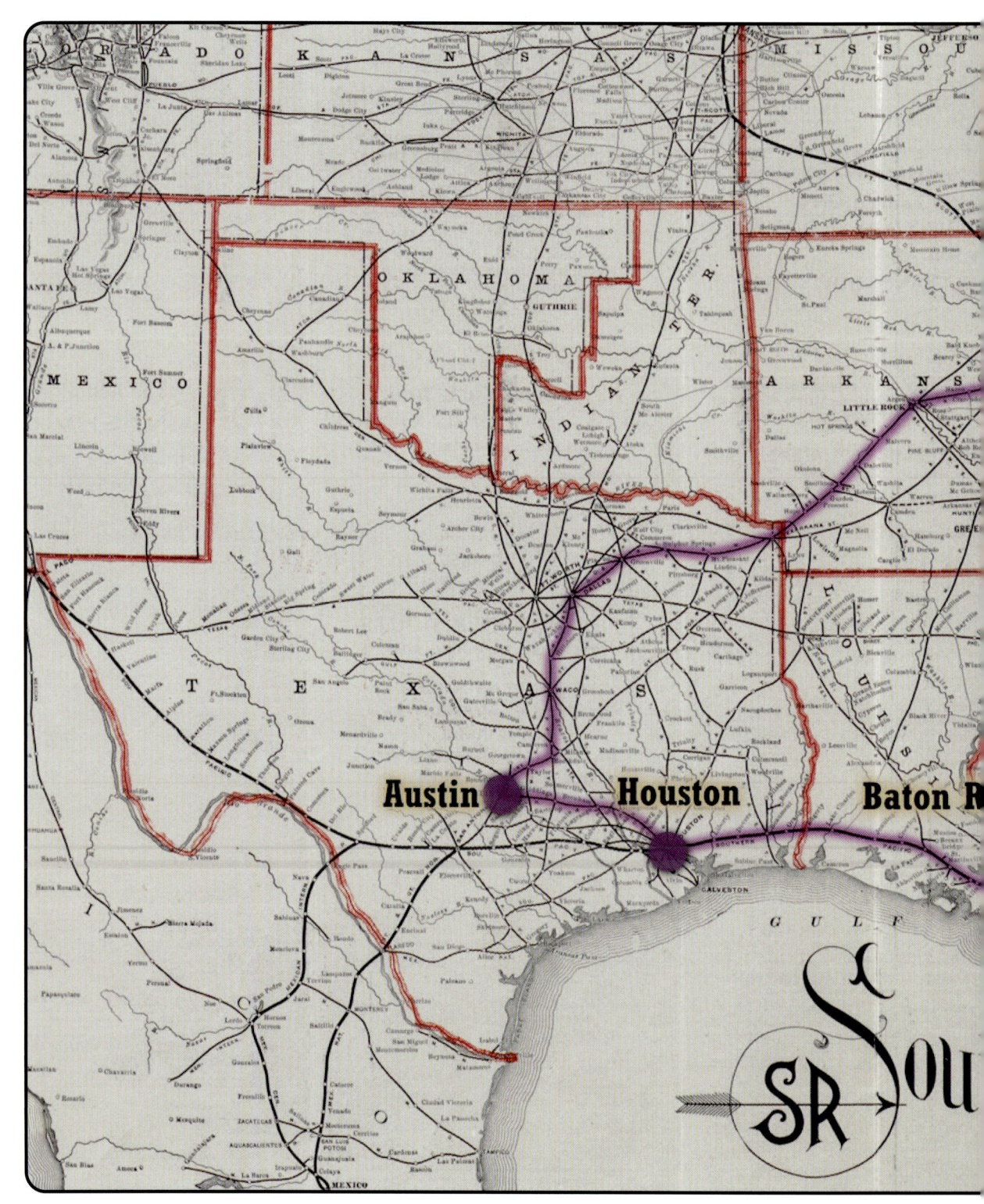

Above: 2,500-mile railroad route for famous road trip; art by Z-Axis

Memphis

Sewanee

New Orleans

Railway

AND CONNECTIONS

80 | UNRIVALED: SEWANEE 1899

THE ROAD TRIP

"My contention is the players of today could not go back to the time of 1899 and travel 2,500 miles and play five games in six days without their comforts that they enjoy today, which are largely gained by the blood, sweat, and tears and perseverance and ingenuity of all those players that preceded them." —Kent Stephens

Three days after the Southwestern Presbyterian game, it was time for the most daunting road trip in college football history. Lea's schedule called for the team to depart Sewanee on Monday, November 6, and travel to Austin, Texas, for a game on Thursday, November 9. Then, the team would play four more games in five days, traveling to Houston, New Orleans, Baton Rouge, and Memphis with only one day of rest.

"Lea's not thinking about the history books. He's thinking about maintaining the program at Sewanee." —Barnhart

Warbler Wilson later recalled, "I don't know if any of us thought about or if anything was said about we might be making American Sports History. We all realized we were up against the best teams in the south and that it would be a tough schedule, but I never saw or ran into any indication that all of us didn't have any thought but that we could and would win." [37]

Apparently, some objections were raised by faculty members about how much class time the players would miss. Shortly before the team was set to depart for its road trip, the student newspaper addressed some of the naysayers: "We understand there has been ... discussion—and some adverse criticism—as to the advisability of prolonged football trips in general, and our prospective Texas trip in particular. Some people of that unsavory class known as 'croakers' delight in compiling statistics about the number of recitations the team will miss in telling how disastrous to all system and organization in classwork a ten-days' absence from the Mountain must be, in counting up the number of students we will thereby lose, because their dear mamas will not send them to a school where discipline is so lax and holidays given for such trifling foolishness as football .... We are going on the Texas trip, the men are going to enjoy it and come back with renewed vigor for classwork, the fame of our university will be spread abroad in that land ... ." [38]

The student newspaper recorded: "This precious cargo of football grit and muscle was shipped via the N., C. & St. L. Railway, on the afternoon of November 6. They and two barrels of Tremlett Spring water were stored away in a special sleeper that was waiting for them at Cowan. This sleeper served the team as a lodging-house during the whole trip. It couldn't come up the mountain, on account of the sharp curves in the track on this Tracy City Branch." [39]

The team had an exhilarating send-off when many of the student body, faculty, and townspeople cheered them as they embarked on the Mountain Goat to start their momentous journey. The crowd gave them resounding cheers as they left, such as:

The team on the road trip consisted of 18 players, Luke Lea, Coach Suter, and Cal Burrows. (Accounts differ on whether there was a second African-American trainer on the trip.) An important aspect of this trip is that Luke Lea had the foresight to have two barrels of spring water from Tremlett Springs in Sewanee stored on the sleeper train. Sanitation at that time was not a given, and he wanted to ensure that the team had fresh, healthy water to drink during the long trip. Cal Burrows would likely have been the person tasked with

Left: IRON MEN OF 1899 depart on The Road Trip. **Above:** Portion of Sewanee cheer sheet celebrating 1899 season

81 | THE SEASON

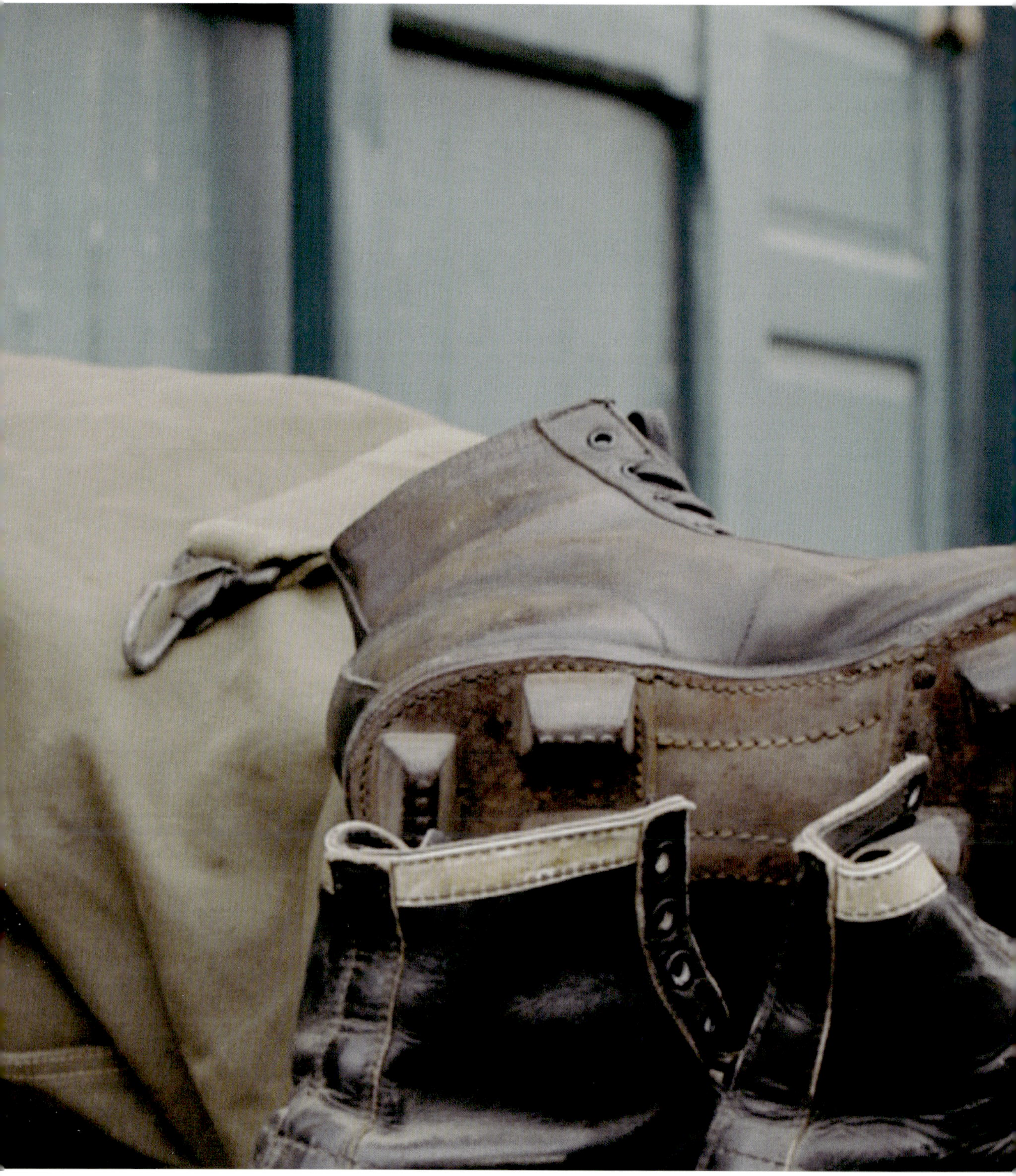

getting the water from Tremlett Springs into the barrels and the barrels onto the train for the trip.

"It sounds like a small thing, but it's not, that he would take the local water with them on a trip like this because the ability to get clean water was not a given in 1899 when you went on the road. … Logistically, given the communication tools that were available then, it's incredible that he was able to pull it off." —Barnhart

It has been noted of these African-American trainers: "We may think that having Tremlett Springs water is a great thing, but that's because we're not carrying that water, and we're not having to do the laundry, wash the uniforms. We're not having to carry all the suitcases and the equipment. They are there and doing that visible—but to us invisible—labor that enabled these men to be made seemingly of iron." —Register

The train trip got off to an inauspicious beginning that threatened to derail the team before it played Texas. After they departed for Texas, Lea discovered that they had left all the cleats at the train station. "The story of how manager Luke Lea, without even letting the team know it was missing, managed to have the equipment catch up with them at U of Texas in Austin is a saga in itself. Luke Lea managed to get the equipment to Austin, Texas simply by using the utmost ingenuity. He discovered that the equipment had been forgotten shortly after the team, in the special car, had been connected to the main line of the N.C. & St. L. North of Cowan, Tennessee. When he reached Nashville he sent a dispatch back to Sewanee c/o the station master instructing that the equipment should be put on the next train, to go via express. Checking the schedule and railroad time tables with which he had been furnished, he then wired an alumnus in Nashville to meet the train, transfer the equipment across town in the middle of the night, and put it on another train instead of waiting until the next day when a dray would have moved the equipment by daylight. At Memphis and at one other point along the route, he had an alumnus meet the train, check the equipment, and make a transfer which saved a few hours. The equipment finally arrived shortly after the team did in Austin." [40]

Luke Lea's daughter, Laura Knox, later commented: "He didn't say a word to anybody on the team. I don't think anybody ever was aware that there was a close call about that."

Left: Cleats left at Cowan Train Depot (re-creation for film)

Texas

THURSDAY, NOVEMBER 9
Varsity Athletic Field
Austin, Texas

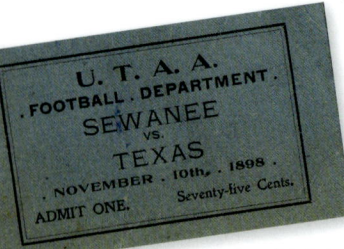

GAME 5

This was the first game of the road trip. In 1898, Sewanee had beaten Texas 5 to 0 in Austin. Texas asked for a rematch and, to entice Sewanee to travel to Austin again, guaranteed Sewanee $750.

Nevertheless, going all the way to Austin, Texas, was very expensive, which is why Lea set up the remaining games on the way back to help pay for the trip.

Texas prepared a football program for the game and included in the program several songs composed about Texas versus Sewanee and set to popular music tunes.

On the opening drive, Texas went 80 yards to Sewanee's 15-yard line. At that point, Sewanee alumnus Pop Atkins waived a fistful of money, saying Texas would not score in the game. He had many takers, and Atkins came very close to losing the bet, but Sewanee held Texas scoreless to win 12-0.

"In 1954, my grandfather received a letter from a gentleman named James Young out of New York City in which he said the following: 'I well remember Simkins' marvelous punting, his long beautiful spirals, the line plunging, and the marvelous teamwork of the Sewanee players, who acted as though they had played the game for many years together.'" —Ralph Black III

Luke Lea sent a telegram after the game which read "To: Sewanee Purple: Sewanee 12, Texas, nothing. Seibels and Simkins, and all the men, played great ball. Crowd not especially large. Features: Sewanee's superb defense on her third yard line and first down. Game played in Texas territory. Men in good fix." [41]

Lea's telegram, however, omitted a crucial event in the first half of the game. As Seibels later recalled, "I suffered a fractured rib and a bad gash above my eye and still bear evidence of the scar." [42] Seibels refused to come out of the game. He went to the sidelines, and they put plaster of Paris on the wound. Remarkably, he continued to play for the entire game.

The *Austin Daily Statesman* reported: "The most painful one was the injury sustained by Capt. Seibles [sic] of the Sewanee team, who had his head badly cut and he bled like a hog. He would not quit the game, however, continuing to play to such good advantage that he secured the credit of both touchdowns. He came out of the game in rather a bloody condition, however." [43]

Kirk Herbstreit has observed, "They would do anything to continue to play football. I think there was a real pride about these players continuing to deal with injuries. It was just a very, very different time and a different place."

The night of the Texas game, the Sewanee players were invited to the University of Texas German Club for a dance. The Purple noted: "They went, of course, but could only stay long enough to discover how much they wished they could stay longer." [44]

Years later, Ralph Black in a letter to Ditty Seibels said, "The Swanee [sic] folks and us so happy and hilarious over our victory, the fine dance beautiful Texas gals, the curfew at ten off to Houston in our Tourist sleeper, etc., the care to drink only out of our Tremlett Spring water barrel." [45]

...Official... Souvenir Program
Texas vs. Sewanee
November 9, 1899.
Athletic Field, Austin, Texas.

L. BETHEA, R.T. '98.   HART, Captain '99.   SEIBLES, Captain, SEWANEE.

Air—"Clementine."

Oh! the weeping and the wailing
Of the vanquished S'wanee boys,
Makes the heart grow sick and fainting
In the midst of all our joys.

CHORUS:
Farewell, Seibles, farewell, Seibles,
Farewell, S'wanee football team.
Thou art lost and gone forever
Under Vars'ty's mighty stream.

We are weary of the boasting
Of that little college team.
They will think when 'Varsity ends them
Life is but an empty dream.

Cade Bethea and Hart and Keller
Overshine old Seible's gang.
Cole and Russ and Schreiner lead them
Where they suffer torture's pang.
—LITTLE SHAVER.

HULLABALOO.

Hullabaloo! Hooray! Hooray!
Hullabaloo! Hooray! Hooray!
Hooray! Hooray!
'Varsity! 'Varsity! U. T. A.

Field Officials.

VARSITY–SEWANEE
......Foot Ball Game......
ATHLETIC FIELD,
Austin, Texas.

Referee, MURRAY, A. & M. Coach, of Pennsylvania State College.
Umpire, BLACKLOCK of Sewanee and Texas.
Linesmen, CRESSON for Texas, KIRBY SMITH for Sewanee.

Game called at 3:15 P. M. and will consist of two twenty minute halves.

SEWANEE 12, VARSITY 0

SUCH WAS THE SCORE MADE BY THE FOOTBALL GAME OF YESTERDAY.

AN IMMENSE CROWD OUT

THE VISITORS HAD PLENTY OF FRIENDS, WHO WERE IN EVIDENCE AT ALL TIMES.

AN INTENSELY EXCITING GAME

The Home Team Went Down in Defeat, But They Snatched Glory From It By the Excellency of Their Work—Individual Work.

Sewanee 12–Texas 0.

Such was the official score of last afternoon's game between the Sewanee University team and the first eleven of the Texas University. It wasn't that it doesn't tell the whole tale by long odds. It does not convey to the public the enthusiasm of the large crowd witnessing the hotly contested game, nor the wildly interesting and exciting plays that were made. The story of that would fill columns, and when completed would not tell the all. From the very outset the 'Varsity team were considered to have the worst of it in weight, skill and experience, but the game had not progressed many minutes when it was clearly shown that the 'Varsity boys were going to give the visitors a run for their money, and such they certainly, did before the game was over.

There was an immense crowd in attendance. They came pouring in from every section of the city and country. They were here from all the neighboring towns, and a number came from Houston and Dallas to see the game. Long before the hour announced for the game, there must have been fully 3,000 people in the grounds, either taking seats and stand or occupying positions along the line in carriages. They were there, highly bedecked in colors. 'Varsity colors, one might have expected, predominated, but the visitors had a number of loyal admirers who wore their colors with all pride feeling due the occasion. The game in itself was something worth viewing. The visitors and their came camp forth with all the concomitants of their sporting knowledge. Were long they were told that the Texas boys were going to meet them a strong tussle, and most certainly did. The game was played with plenty of ginger from the very starting. True, the visitors opened up, and taking the ball up into the 'Varsity territory proceeded to force it with rapid strides dangerously close to 'Varsity goal. An opportune kick, however, brought the ball back into near the center of the field. Thrice was this performance repeated, and again, and not until then did the visitors manage by dint of great work to make a touchdown. The first half lacked only a few minutes of expiring when this first touchdown was made, and there was no more scoring done in the first half. In the second half the 'Varsity boys went forth with a firm determination to do or die. They fought such a game as has seldom been witnessed on these grounds before. They executed every movement that could gain them any vantage ground. They ere long showed that they were making excellent progress. The ball was carried up the field in excellent shape, and was gradually brought so close to the visitors' goal that the entire assemblage was on tip toe. The 'Varsity boys fought with all the vigor of desperation, and managed to get within seven yards of the visitors' goal, when they lost the ball. Here the visitors arose to the occasion and fought the battle of the day. They managed by dint of great physical exertion and hard playing to get the ball away from their goal, and then a kick placed it in the field, where a bitter contest was fought. Once away from their goal, the visitors seemed to become possessed of a tigerlike ferocity, and fairly fought their way down the field to the 'Varsity's goal. They fought their way through the center, sometimes by a straight buck, sometimes by huddle movements, but in each event they managed to gain a few yards. In this manner they pushed their way down the field with only seven minutes time in which to play. The 'Varsity goal was ere long within reaching distance. The last stand was taken and the ground bitterly contested, but all to no purpose. The visitors secured their touchdown and kicked the goal just as the time was up, and thus ended the game, with the score of 12 to 0 in their favor. It was generally conceded by every one as one of the most spirited and interesting games ever played on the local field. Interest was kept at fever heat throughout, and too much praise can not be accorded the two teams for their most excellent work. They both seemed to fight with the vigorousness of wild animals to snatch success from the contest, and while the 'Varsity went down, they did so in such defeat that they are glorious notwithstanding it.

The game, throughout was attended with the very best of decorum; there was not the slightest wrangling or unpleasantness. The visitors proved themselves perfect gentlemen and played a strictly straight game. There

the game. The most painful one was the injury sustained by Capt. Seibles of the Sewanee team, who had his head badly cut and he bled like a hog. He would not quit the game, however, continuing to play to such good advantage that he secured the credit of both touchdowns. He came out of the game in rather a bloody condition, however. Russ of the 'Varsity team received some back bruises, but nothing serious. The write-up of the game follows:

THE GAME.

The game, though it resulted in the defeat of the home team, was well worth seeing, and will rank as one of the great games of the Texas gridiron. Sewanee won, and did it fairly, but the Texans have no reason to be ashamed of the showing they made. They played a good game and held the visitors to two touch downs, besides once threatening their goal, and to such an extent that it seemed that nothing could prevent a Texas touchdown. It was in the second half. The ball went to 'Varsity in the middle of the field and by steady work she carried it down the field until Sewanee's 7-yard line was reached. At this point she lost the ball by a narrow margin, and with it lost her only good chance to score. Keller had just made it the first down by smashing through tackle for two yards. Cole was then called on but Seibles broke through the 'Varsity line and tackled him for a loss. On the next two plays, 'Varsity failing to gain the necessary five yards, the ball went to Sewanee.

Sewanee has a splendid team and her backs are among the best that have ever played on the 'Varsity field. They showed their good work by repeatedly breaking through the Texas line, sometimes making from twenty to thirty yards. They were quick and aggressive but seemed to depend entirely on their ability to force the line for gains, as the only kind of play they attempted was unsuccessful. Their line was also strong but the Texas warded with ten yards and then gets ten more on a double pass. Sewanee continues to smash the 'Varsity line, the next two plays being made against left tackle and left guard, and net the Tennesseans twelve yards. Seibles then gains five yards through 'Varsity's right tackle but fails to gain the next play against centre. Simkins is next tried against centre, but with the same result, and Sewanee failing to gain on the third attempt, the ball goes to 'Varsity on downs. The Texas men now quickly carry the ball toward the Sewanee goal, by sending Bethea through right tackle for ten yards and then after two fruitless attempts at forcing through centre, Keller punts thirty yards to Jones, who returns with it fifteen yards and run out of bounds at 'Varsity's 50 yard line. Sewanee resumes her bucking tactics, sending Seibles against left guard for three yards, Simkins through the same place for eight yards, and then five on yard. Grey smashes left guard and gains one yard and then tries the same place with a three yard gain. Simkins takes his turn at advancing the ball and puts a hole between left tackle and guard, through which he makes three yards and then repeats the performance through left guard and centre, with a four yard gain. The 'Varsity men at this point capture the ball on a fumble on their 20-yard line and after advancing it eight yards on line bucks, they resort to a punt which goes forty yards and nets them 30. Sewanee again hammers at their opponents' line, but make only small gains and soon lose the ball to 'Varsity on an off-side play, but immediately recapture it on a fumble. 'Varsity stiffens up and holds the Tennesseans on downs on 'Varsity's 37-yard line. Here the Texas backs tear through the visitors line for good gains and advance twelve yards around left end. Hart is given the ball and goes through the opposite guard for five yards. 'Varsity makes an off-side play and forfeits the ball and then is penalized for holding. Simkins is sent between guard and tackle for thirty yards and again brings the ball dangerously near the 'Varsity goal. He again tries the same place for four yards and then again for three more thus placing the ball on Texas' 7-yard line. Seibles makes a touchdown on the next play through left tackle and guard, and Pierce kicks a goal, making a score of six to nothing in favor of Sewanee after 25 minutes of play.

'Varsity again kicks off, this time for forty yards, and Sewanee only returns five yards. She then opens up left guard and tackle and Seibles goes through for thirty-five yards. The next three attempts are directed against the line, but net her very small gains and Sewanee is forced to punt. This is caught by Russ on 'Varsity's 35-yard line. Keller of the 'Varsity smashes Sewanee's left tackle for fifteen yards, and Shreiner gains three yards more through the opposite tackle. Bethea is next given the ball and gains one yard through right tackle; then Keller punts Sewanee's ball. She begins to hammer the 'Varsity line and has the ball on 'Varsity's 40-yard line when the first half is over.

The second half begins with 'Varsity in possession of the ball. Simkins of Sewanee kicks off thirty yards to Russ and Tennessee net forty yards. Shreiber makes three yards through right tackle. Bethea hits right tackle for two more and again for five yards. Cole next tries centre but fails to gain and Keller punts forty yards to Seibles, who returns it thirty-five, a gain for Texas of five yards. Cole again is sent against centre without result and then Shreiner makes his usual gain through right tackle. Keller sends the ball through the air four yards to Simkins, who brings it back twenty yards to the centre of the field.

Sewanee then again resorts to a punt and this time sends it thirty-five yards to Russ, who brings it back eight yards. Huss Bethea and Shreiner make small gains in the next two plays and the third play is a mass on tackle by which Keller gains three yards. Bethea is called on to try tackle for a gain, and he advances the ball three yards. 'Varsity here fumbles but retains the ball and Keller punts thirty yards to Seibles who catches the ball for a fair kick from Sewanee's 45-yard line. The kick nets thirty-five yards, but 'Varsity gets the ball, but immediately loses it on account of a 'Varsity man holding. Seibles punts thirty-five yards and Russ makes a magnificent 25-yard run up the field. The Texans here begin to carry the ball down the field by repeated hammering at the line; until they are on Sewanee's 7-yard line. It looked like a touch down, but Sewanee broke through on the next play and tackled Cole for a loss and captured the ball on downs. The visitors pierce the Texas line time and again and soon have the ball in the middle of the field, when Simkins smashes through the 'Varsity line, gets past Russ and makes a 30-yard run before being tackled. Sewanee next tries a mass play on left tackle for a three yard gain, and again on the same place for eight yards, but loses the ball on downs on 'Varsity's 25-yard line. Keller gains three yards and Monteith makes five yards on line plays, but the ball goes to Sewanee on a fumble and she resumes her mass plays on centre until the ball is on 'Varsity's 4-1-2... the ball. Grey plunges at the 'Varsity centre but makes only one yard; then Seibles tries right tackle and gains four yards. Grey is next sent against the left of the 'Varsity line and is re-

---

> The most painful one was the injury sustained by Capt. Seibles of the Sewanee team, who had his head badly cut and he bled like a hog. He would not quit the game, however, continuing to play to such good advantage that he secured the credit of both touchdowns. He came out of the game in rather a bloody condition, however.

Left: Texas team 1899 **Above:** Texas prepared a football program for the game and included in the program several songs composed about Texas vs. Sewanee and set to popular music tunes.
Right and highlighted copy: AUSTIN DAILY STATESMAN, Friday, November 10, 1899

85 | THE SEASON

Above: Sewanee vs. Texas: one of the two known photographs of a Sewanee game in 1899

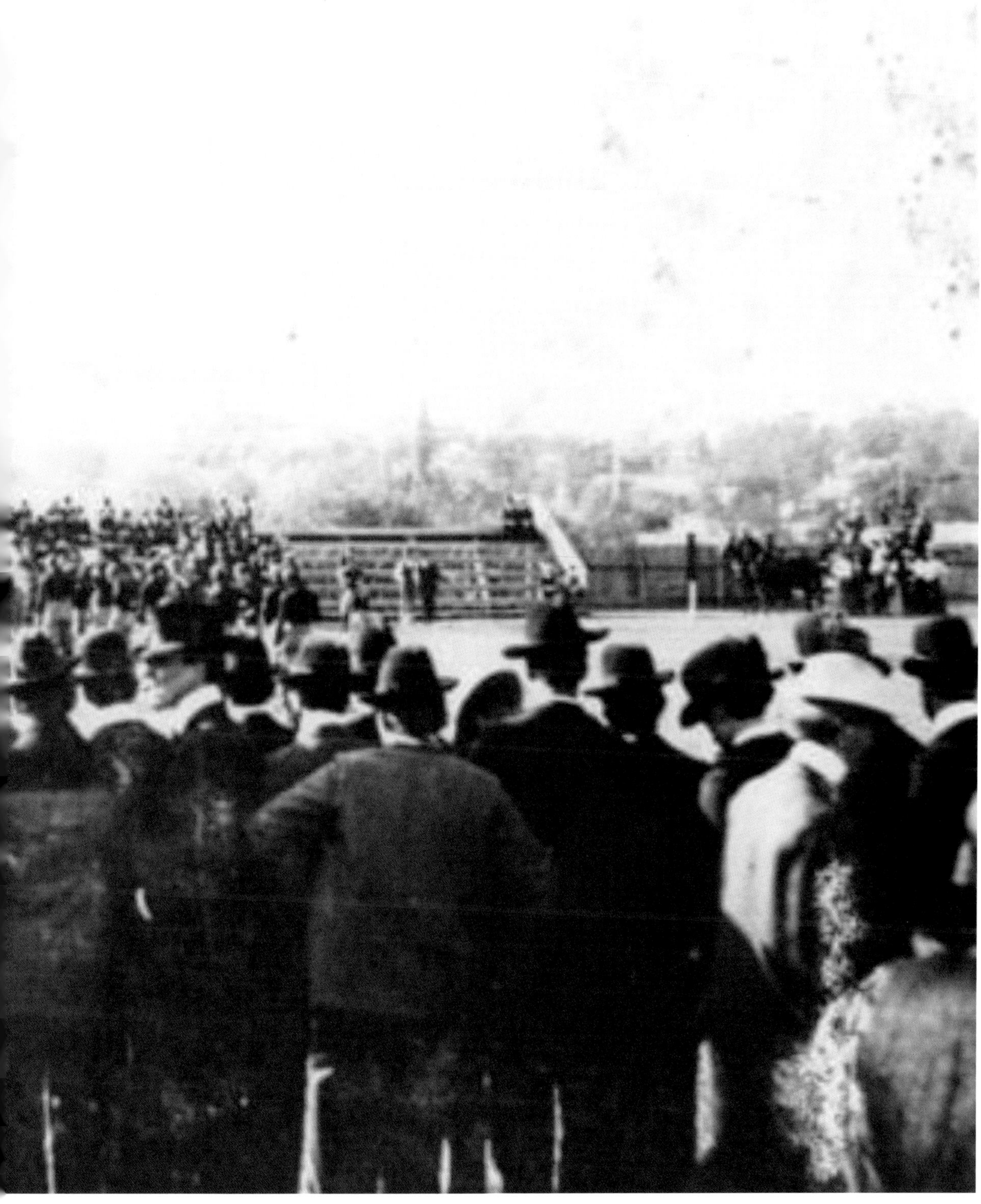

Above: FIRST DOWN, Sewanee vs. Texas 1899

89 | THE SEASON

Texas A&M

FRIDAY, NOVEMBER 10
Herald Park
Houston, Texas

After an all-night train ride, Sewanee faced Texas A&M in Houston on Friday, November 10. The *Bryan Morning Eagle* reported, "A young man in a football sweater sent a telegram this morning. His eye was closed by a lump of no mean proportions. A bystander wrote it for him. It was to a girl and read 'No-body hurt.'"[46]

Despite the gash in his head from the Texas game, Ditty Seibels played the whole game with plaster over the cut.

At one point in the game, an A&M runner rushed around right end and was on his way to score when Simkins ran him down with a crushing tackle.

Sewanee prevailed by a score of 10 to 0 and then rode all night to New Orleans.

GAME 6

Above: Texas A&M team in 1900 and a ticket to the match **Right:** BRYAN MORNING EAGLE—description of game with telegram message "No-body hurt"

90 | UNRIVALED: SEWANEE 1899

Eagle.

NOVEMBER 12, 1899.   Price 5 Cents.

m Tennessee were up against dest team so far met in their us march throughout the south, ely say. The college boys were green and skittish, so the game went against them; the endurance, too, shown by Sewanee helped them to turn the scale. The spectators were pleased nobody was seriously hurt, there was no serious bickering and no prize fights. Football has had a lift in Houston through this game.

Druesdow, of Houston, is trying to arrange a game between this city and the A. & M. Promising material abounds here.

"Babe" Astin, of college, played football for all there was in it—even until his clothing had well nigh gone from him in shreds. His nickname is well deserved; he's the "Switch Engine of the H. & B. V., because you can't stop him."

Coach Senter, of Sewanee said today's was the seventh game won, no score having been made against his team, 179 points having been piled up by Sewanee against nothing by their opponents. He says the A. & M. college team

A young man in a football sweater sent a telegram this morning. His eye was closed by a lump of no mean proportions. A bystander wrote it for him. It was to a girl, and read: "Nobody hurt."

Hotel Arrivals.

EXCHANGE

A P Wilson, Houston; Abe Edel, Cincinnati; H O Shepard and wife, Chicago; S P Porter, Saratoga; I N Kime, Toledo; R L Henry, Waco;

WILL HOLD HIS PLAC

Congressman Smith Will Not Resig til He Is Made Governor.

Baltimore, Nov. 11.— A prece having been established in the ca Governor Hill, who a short time held a seat in the United States as well as the governship, John W Smith, the newly elected Democ governor of Maryland, will, it is keep his seat in congress until his auguration as governor, the se Monday in January next. He elected to congress from the firs trict last November. Mr. Smith representative of the tidewater se of Maryland, is deeply interested i river and harbor bill and he also w his opinion on the Democratic presi tal nomination to become known is a sound money Democrat. The ernor must decide when a special tion for congressman shall be he the district. The probable Democ candidates for these nomination ex-Governor Elihu Jackson, ex-Cong man Joshua W. Miles, State Senato F. Applegate and ex-State Se Thomas A. Smith.

GUARD ATTACKED.

He Is Considerably Used Up, but tured One of His Prisoners.

San Antonio, Nov. 11.— A terrible between a sentinel and two mili convicts seeking to escape occurred Fort Sam Houston on the western

Above: SIMKINS PREVENTS TOUCHDOWN, Sewanee vs. Texas A&M

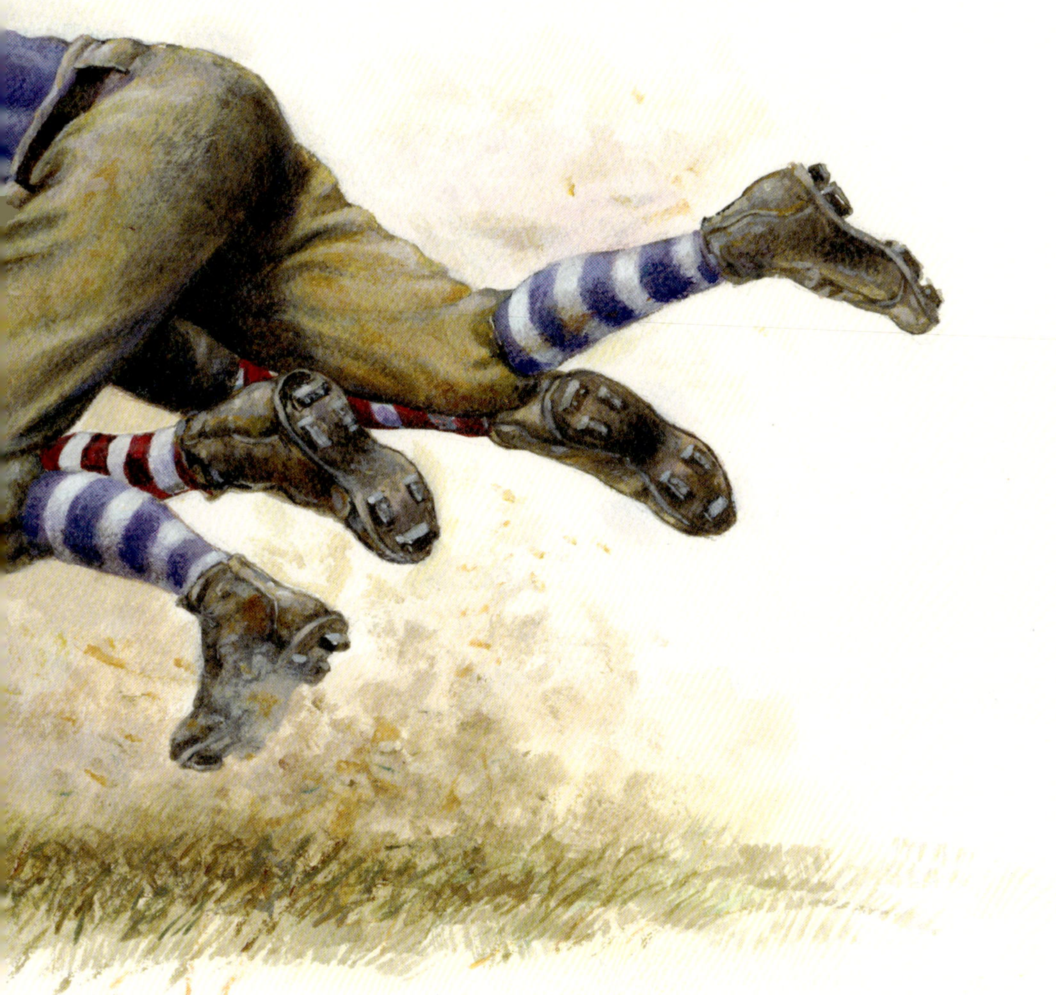

Tulane

SATURDAY, NOVEMBER 11
Crescent City Base Ball Park
New Orleans, Louisiana

The third game on the road saw Sewanee in New Orleans to face Tulane.

Lea sent the following telegram to Vice Chancellor Wiggins after the game: "Sewanee Twenty three, Tulane nothing. Gray, Kilpatrick, Simpkins [sic], Bolling, Jones, and Wilson played best game. Notwithstanding that this was Sewanee's third game. Men showed better physical condition than Tulane. All well." [47]

The Tulane newspaper reported on their loss by observing: "Then, too, we must remember that the Sewanee boys have the advantage of being strengthened by the exhilarating mountain air that blows around their University and as the Sewanee students have rights in their University and have Dormitories … there is to be a great college spirit fostered in the hearts of the Sewanee students." [48]

The team had dinner at Victor's and then went to the Tulane Theater to see "Rupert of Hentzau."

"I know they spent one night in New Orleans, but I think Luke would not let them go out on the town. They had to attend a play. One of the characters was dressed in purple, and it aroused the team so much because that was their team colors. They stood up and gave the Sewanee cheer, and the whole audience went kind of nuts." —K. Seibels

The Sewanee cheer:
"Rip 'em up, tear 'em up,
Leave 'em in the lurch.
Down with the heathen, Up with the Church.
Yea, Sewanee's right!"

On Sunday, November 12, the team had a day of rest, toured a sugar plantation, and may have gone sailing on Lake Pontchartrain.

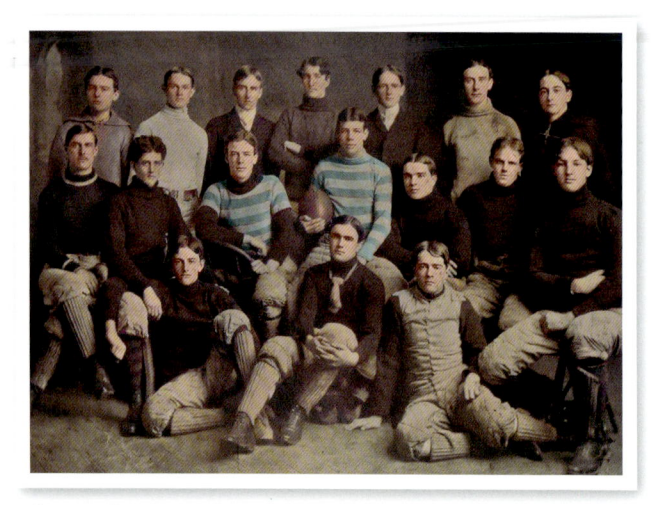

GAME 7

Above: Tulane team 1899

Olive and Blue

Vol. IV. NO. 7.   TULANE UNIVERSITY, NEW ORLEANS, THURSDAY, NOVEMBER 16, 1899.   FIVE CENTS PER COPY.

G 101
BALCONY
TULANE
GOOD ONLY ON
SATURDAY EVE'G
NOV'BR 11
..GLOBE TICKET COMPANY..

[Tu]lane Defeated by Sewanee in a very Exciting Game by the Score of 23–0.

[L]ast Saturday afternoon, before [one] of the largest crowds ever as[sem]bled on Tulane Campus, the [var]sity went down in defeat before [the] boys who wear the purple, by a [sco]re of 23–0.

Although the score was large it [in] no way indicates that Sewanee [ha]d an easy time of it. On the con[tra]ry, every gain they made was [stu]bbornly contested, Tulane's de[fen]se, at times being equal if not [su]perior to Sewanee's.

Tulane's defeat is attributed [ma]inly to inexperience. Of course [th]ere is no use denying that Sewa[n]ee has one of the best, if not the [be]st team in the South, as her long [st]ring of victories indicates, but [w]e feel sure had Tulane played the [s]ame number of games as has Sewanee, the score would have been different.

Although beaten, Tulane can well feel proud of her team. It was their first game this season, and splendidly did they play it, at no time letting up in fierceness of play even when a high score was rolled up against them. The second [part] of the game is an evidence [of this] fact, for in it Sewanee made [only] one touchdown, while in the [first] they made three.

The Sewanee boys arrived [Sat]urday morning in their priva[te car] over the Southern Pacific, and [were] met at the depot by the Comm[ittee] of students appointed for that [pur]pose. The Committee boarde[d the] train and accompanied the tea[m to] the Illinois Central Depot and [then] escorted them to the Grune[wald] Hotel where breakfast was se[rved].

The Tennesseeans decided to [re]main in their private car du[ring] their stay. Sewanee appeare[d on] the Campus at 3:30, and Tula[ne]

concerned, but it was too warm for fast foot-ball.

Although the game was called for 3.30 p. m., it was past 4 o'clock before the two teams lined up. By that time the grand stand was well filled with a very large and fashionable audience, while a large number of persons took advantage of the side lines so as to watch the game better. A conservative estimate would place the number of people present at about 1000.

While the Olive and Blue predominated, there was no lack of supporters of the Purple, as was evidenced by the rousing welcome given to Sewanee when she appeared on the field. When the Varsity arrived a few minutes later, in their new uniforms, they were given a tremendous ovation.

The length of the halves having been previously decided upon to be 25 and 20 minutes respectively, the coin was tossed and Captain Eshleman won, choosing the south goal and giving the ball to Sewanee. At a few minutes past 4 o'clock, Umpire Parker blew his whistle and the game commenced.

Kilpatrick, of Sewanee, kicked off for 40 yards. The ball was [out of bounds?] the Varsity was too eager and got off side, giving the ball to Sewanee who sent Kilpatrick through the line for a 20 yard buck and a touchdown. Time, 5.45 minutes. Pearce kicked an easy goal. Score 6—0.

Eshleman kicked off for 40 yards and Simkins ran it back 10 before he was beautifull[y tackled by Esh]leman. Simkins [then got] the ball rolling [around the end.] Post was there a[nd tackled the] Varsity. Stear[ns tried a] tackle around ta[ckle but was] plunged through [for 5 yards] and Owens we[nt around end] for 3 more, L[evert, on good] interference, go[t around for] 20 yards. Stea[rns plunged] out of opposit[e tackle and] bucked straigh[t through, but] Eshleman tried [a trick play but] find no holes. [Owens went] yard around ta[ckle but] could not gai[n. On a buck] the ball went [to Tulane.] Simkins kicke[d 30 yards to Pearce] who fumbled, [Sewanee recovered] the ball. W[ith good interfer]ence, Gray [got around for] yards and b[roke loose on] the next play [for a]

Then, too, we must remember that the Sewanee boys have the advantage of being strengthened by the exhilarating mountain air that blows around their University and as the Sewanee students have rights in their University and have Dormitories, instead of living at home and attending College as day scholars, there is to be a great college spirit fostered in the hearts of the Sewanee

---

The Game with Texas

COME ONE, COME ALL.

Next Monday at 3:30 o'clock the 'Varsity is to play the University of Texas on the college campus. The game promises to be a most interesting and exciting one in every [way...]

TULANE DEFEATED BY SEWANEE.

pass, failed to gain but, on the same trick, Bolling was able to get 5 yards. Gray bucked for 5 on side of the line and Kilpatrick repeated the dose on his side. Gray got around the end for 3 more before he was downed. Here Sewanee fumbled but retained the ball. Gray hammered 2½ out of the Varsity's tackle and tried the same thing on the next play, but he was beautifully tackled by Levert with a loss. Simkins took 7 out of the center before he was stopped by Eshleman. The ball was now on Tulane's 10. yard line, when Sewanee fumbled and Tulane secured the ball. Levert on a trick gained a yard, and bucked for the same amount on the next play. Eshleman kicked 30 yards to Simkins. Sewanee sent Gray through the tackle for 5 yards and gained 3 yards on the next play by a quarter-back trick. Gray fumbled but saved the ball and made 3 yards. Gray got through the line for 5 yards around the end, and Kilpatrick got 2 on the same kind of play. The ball was on Tulane's 5 yard line and Sewanee sent Gray through on a buck for a touchdown. Time 22.50 minutes. Pearce missed the goal, making the score 17–0.

Eshleman made a beautiful kick of 50 yards and Simkins brought it back 15. Gray cleared the end twice for 3 and 1 yards respectively. Jones, on a trick got away from the crowd and ran 28 yards before was beautifully tackled by Levert from behind. On a quarter back trick, Wilson got 15 yards, [be]fore he was downed by Post. [Gr]ay bucked and was heavily thrown [by] Eshleman with a loss. The [whi]stle blew before the teams could [lin]e up, the ball being on Tulane's [ya]rd line.

[Be]tween the halves, the coaches [ca]lled their respective teams aside [and g]ave them some good words of [advice.]

SECOND HALF.

[The] second half opened with a [kick of] 25 yards by Eshleman. [The ball was] sure touchdown, but Sewanee's little full-back Simkins was there and nailed him, after he had made 20 yards. Owens failed to gain on the next play so Levert was called in to take the ball and he distinguished himself by a 10 yard buck. Owens got around the end for 2 yards before he was tackled but Levert lost on his adventure around the end. Eshleman kicked for 30 yards to Simkins who fumbled the ball and a Varsity man fell on it. Owens tried a buck but was forced back ½ yard. Stearns also failed to gain so Levert was sent through the line for 4 yards, but as Owens could not gain the required distance on the next down the ball went to Sewanee. Gray gained 8 yards around the end but was hurt in the scrimmage and forced to retire. Hull took his place. Jones on a trick made 35 yards before he was downed. On the next play Hull fumbled but Simkins saved the ball for Sewanee. Kilpatrick got around the end for 2 yards. Here some changes were made in the Varsity Kilpatrick was taken off the end and Westfeldt was put on, but Eshleman getting hurt in the next play, Westfeldt was moved to fullback and Allain Eustis put on the end. Simkins plunged through the Varsity's line for 7 yards. The ball was now on Tulane's 4 yard line and in the next play Kilpatrick carried it over for the third and last touchdown. Time 8 minutes. Pearce kicked the goal, the score being 23–0.

Westfeldt kicked off for 45 yards, but Simkins by fine running recovered 30 yards of it. Sewanee fumbled but retained the ball. Simkins made a poor punt of 25 yards and Tulane secured the ball. Owens got a yard around the end, and Stearns took ten out of the opposite tackle. Owens could not gain around the end but Levert made up for it with a ten yard buck. Post fumbled on the next play but saved the ball. Levert made 4 yards on a pretty buck. Westfeldt [kicked for 30?] yards by grazing tackle, Simkins kicked, and Westfeldt returned the punt, but the exchange netted Sewanee 25 yards. Kilpatrick circled end for 12 yards, and then Jones went 30 yards on a trick play. The gain however was not allowed as the ball was passed before the umpire called play. Hull went around end for 5 yards and Simkins added 3 on a fluke. Simkins was hurt and Brooks was substituted. Kilpatrick failed to gain around end and the game was called on Tulane's 40 yard line.

The playing of the entire Sewanee team was good. It showed the results of long and careful training. Simkins, Kilpatrick, Pearce, and Jones did the best individual work. For Tulane, Levert was easily the star. His line buck was ferocious and his defensive work excellent. Eshleman, Stearns, Owens and Mangum pressed him for the honors of the day.

Box 101, M. D. & L. Exchange.   Phone 210-2

FRANK J. MATTHEW,

PAINTER AND DECORATOR.

HIGH ART WALL PAPER,

1208-1210 CANAL STREET.

NEW ORLEANS, LA.

..Office or Home

Is Incomplete Without

THE TIMES-DEMOCRAT

A Cameo in Printer's Ink.

All the news of both hemispheres embodying a complete history from every field of current events accessible by wire or word.

Daily - - - $12 per year.
Semi-weekly, $1 per year

Talk to your newsdealers or address

The Times-Democrat,
New Orleans, La.

Form No. 1

THE WESTERN UNION

INCORP

21,000 OFFICES IN AMERICA.   CA

This Company TRANSMITS and DELIVERS messages only on conditions li
Errors can be guarded against only by repeating a message back to the sending
transmission or delivery of Unrepeated Messages, beyond the amount of tolls pa
after the message is filed with the Company for transmission.
This is an UNREPEATED MESSAGE, and is delivered by request of the se

THOS. T. ECKERT, Presi

NUMBER	SENT BY	REC'D BY	
47	Da	Ld	3

RECEIVED at 4 20 Pm

Dated New Orleans

To B L Wiggins

Sewanee Twenty thr
Kilpatrick Simpkin
Wilson played best
that this was Sewanee
better physical condition

Above: Lea's telegram to V.C. Wiggins after the Tulane game **Pages 98-99:** UNRIVALED TRAIN TRIP

...ELEGRAPH COMPANY,

...LE SERVICE TO ALL THE WORLD

Paid

Nov 11, 1899

... Chancellor
... anee Tenn

... Tulane nothing. Gray
... Bolling Jones &
... game. Notwithstanding
third game men showed
... than Tulane. All well.

Luke Lea mgr

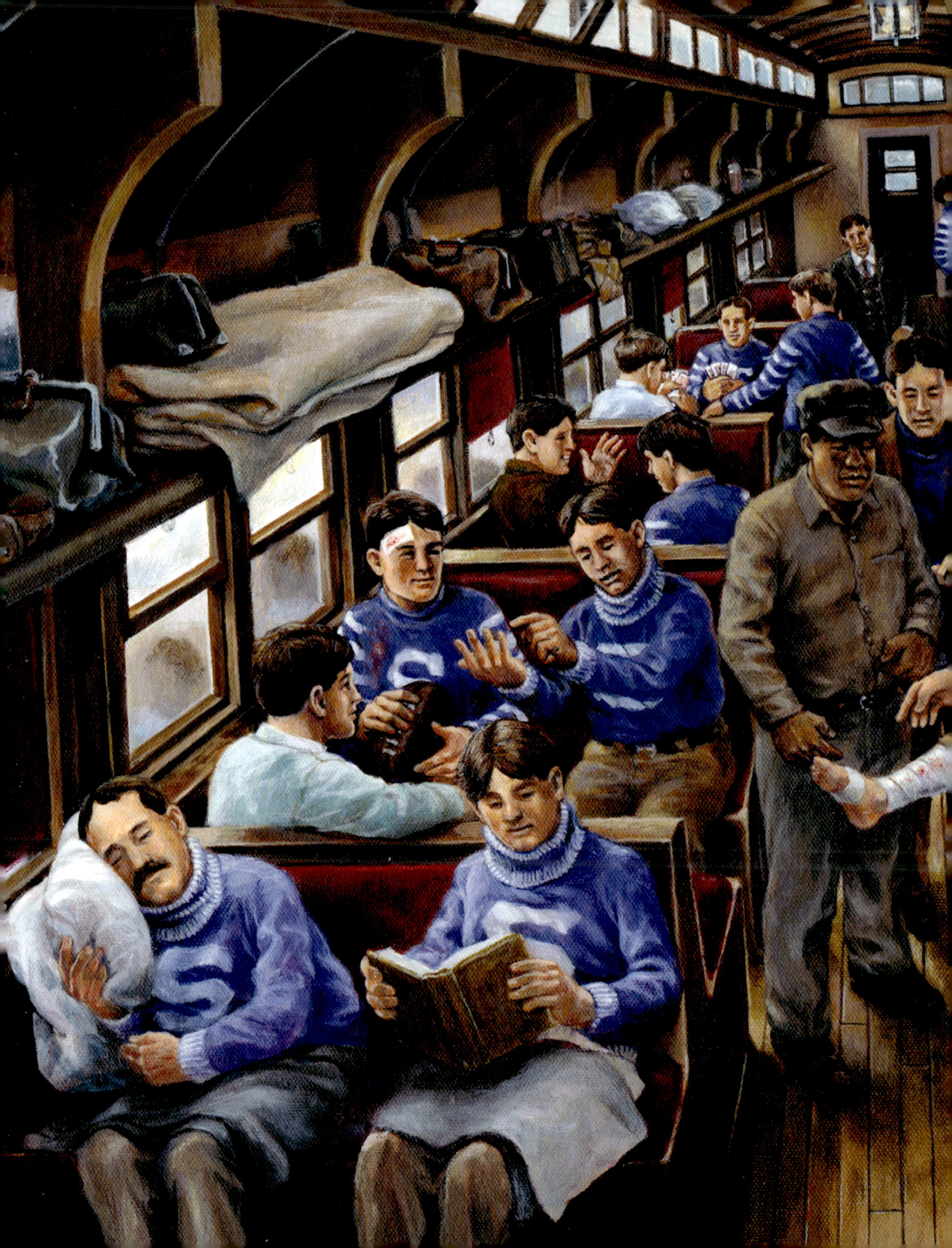

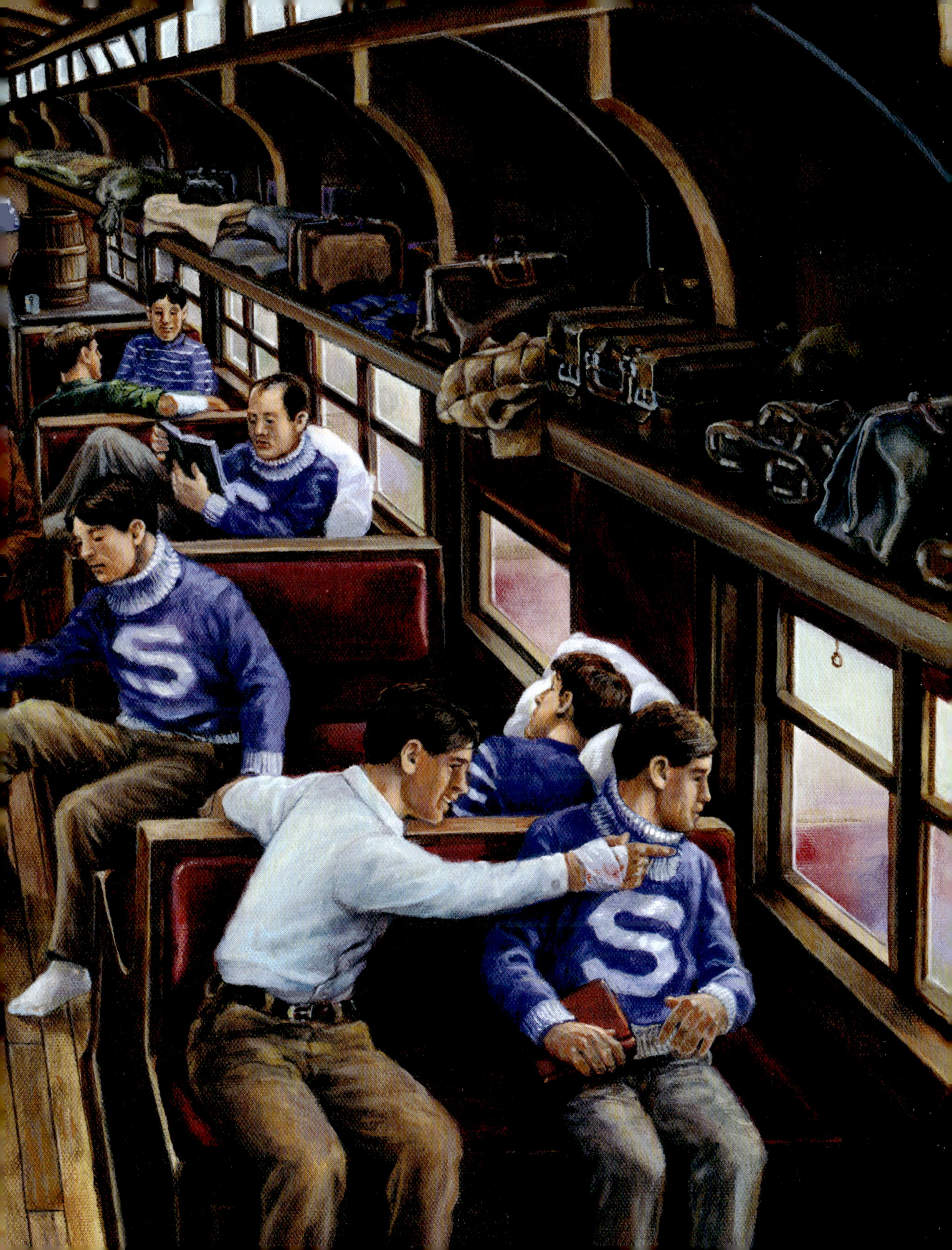

"Vice Chancellor Wiggins insisted that the student athletes maintain respectable grades. That was a risky thing to do for a place that was as small as Sewanee, to insist on academic excellence for athletes. . . . When they came back from that glorious trip, they still had to come back to class, and they had to take exams."

—JERRY SMITH

"While all this is going on, they're having to study. They're having to work at their academics." —Barnhart

LSU

MONDAY, NOVEMBER 13
State Field
Baton Rouge, Louisiana

LSU had a grass field, which the Sewanee players considered a real luxury. *The Sewanee Purple* reported: "Our boys, who practice every afternoon on Hardee Park, with rocks for a gridiron, nearly went to sleep on that nice, soft field every time they were tackled." [49]

Sewanee prevailed 34 to 0.

The LSU newspaper reported on their big loss to Sewanee by noting this: "The features of the game were the beautiful interference and team work of Sewanee and the fine work of her backs, Hull, Kilpatrick and Wilson." [50]

GAME 8

Left: LSU team 1899 **Above:** QUICK KICK, Sewanee vs. LSU

Ole Miss

TUESDAY, NOVEMBER 14
Billings Park
Memphis, Tennessee

GAME 9

After the LSU game, the team boarded the train to travel to Memphis to play Ole Miss for its fifth game in six days. As the team kept winning, newspapers picked up the story and began to see the significance of the amazing train trip.

After yet another all-night train trip, the team arrived in Memphis on Tuesday, November 14. The Ole Miss team was known as the "long-haired knights of the oval from Oxford" [51] because they wore long hair for protection of their heads.

"The Mississippi players objected that some of the Sewanee players had these meager, little leather helmets because, to their mind, honor dictated that you play with long hair and not a helmet." —Prunty

The referee overruled this objection, and the game went forward.

The *Commercial Appeal* reported on the game and noted: "It is only fair for Mississippi to say that several of her best men were on the hospital list. Sewanee's crippled condition offset this, however. … As the bandaged boys in purple took their positions, Coach Suter applied fresh plaster over the cut which Seibels received in the Texas game. The sight of the Sewanee men as they stood ready for the referee's whistle was enough to create a wholesome respect for them. … Sewanee was putting forth a fierce attack and with Coach Suter yelling for them to, 'Tear 'em up!' " [52]

It is obvious from this account that by this time the Sewanee players were beaten up, heavily bandaged, and bone-weary. Despite their wounded condition, however, they prevailed over Ole Miss 12 to 0.

"Think about playing one football game where you are completely exhausted. You get in a tub of ice. You get the kinks worked out, and you're ready to go again on Saturday. Try playing five games in six days." —Jones

Above: Ole Miss team 1899 **Right:** THE COMMERCIAL APPEAL, November 15, 1899 **Pages 106-107:** THE BANDAGED BOYS IN PURPLE

104 | UNRIVALED: SEWANEE 1899

COMMERCIAL APPEAL: MEMPHIS, WEDNESDAY MOR[NING]

THE FIFTH SHUT-OUT

SEWANEE FOOTBALL ELEVEN COMPLETES ITS TOUR.

MISSISSIPPI DIDN'T SCORE

The Game Was Decidedly the Best on the Memphis Gridiron This Season, and One of Which Oxford May Be Proud.

There were no bonfires at Oxford last night, no celebration, no hurrah of any kind by the students of the University of Mississippi.

The football warriors of Oxford, who gained sudden fame a few weeks ago at Citizens' Park, tackled Sewanee at Billings Park yesterday afternoon, and that is why the celebration at Oxford was postponed indefinitely.

Although defeated, the dose which the loyal supporters of "Old M-i-s-s" were forced to take was a very palatable one, and as a result of the gridiron conflict with the collegians from the mountains of Middle Tennessee the adherents of the Ox[ford]... will send the welcome extended the wearers of the purple when they arrive home today.

Best Game of the Season.

Yesterday's contest was the best of the trio of intercollegiate games offered the local public this year. Sewanee used excellent generalship. In the first half Capt. Seibels hammered away at the tackles until Mississippi's ends were drawn in. In the second half, about accomplished, the purple backs swept wide and clear for long runs. Fumbling played an important part in Sewanee's score, and but for the juggling of Kilpatrick and Seibels one, or possibly two, additional touchdowns would have resulted. Suter's trick formations, which the Tennesseans exhibited yesterday, completely smothered and nonplussed the Oxonians. At the delayed pass, great interference and running in the open field Sewanee greatly outclassed her opponents. The maneuvering in the kicking line was about equal, however, but Mississippi's ends were off quicker and down the field in better shape than Sewanee. In all other departments Sewanee excelled.

It is only fair for Mississippi to say that several of her best men were on the hospital list. Sewanee's crippled condition offset this, however.

As usual society showed great interest, and the traps and turnouts were large in numbers and laden with the culture and beauty of Memphis' swell set, which lent picturesqueness to the scene of the gridiron, lined with howling, cheering students and alumni of both universities.

From the result of yesterday's game one thing is certain, that Mississippi has an eleven in which she can feel confident of holding her own against the 'varsity teams in this section. Her old rival, Tulane, the team which Harris G. Collier is coaching, will surely be defeated on Thanksgiving day.

Score, 12 to 0.

The line-up was:

Sewanee.	Positions.	Mississippi.
Sims	Left end	Foster
Jones	Left tackle	Hall
Keyes	Left guard	White
Poole	Center	Wainwright
Claiborne	Right guard	McIntyre
Bolling	Right tackle	Redhead
Pearce, Black	Right end Henry, Montgomery
Wilson	Quarter back	Clapp
Kilpatrick	Left half back	Harvey
Seibels	Right half back	Chandler
Simkins	Full back	Myers

Summaries—Twenty-five and twenty-minute halves were played. Referee, J. W. S. Rhea. Umpire, Wilson Mallory, University of Virginia. Touchdowns, Kilpatrick 2. Goals from touchdowns, Sims 2. Linesmen, Cope and McFarland. Timers, Dabney and Thompson.

THE GAME IN DETAIL.

Mississippi won the toss and chose the south goal, which was favored by a strong wind. As the bandaged boys in purple took their positions, Coach Suter applied fresh plaster over the cut which Seibels received in the Texas game. The sight of the Sewanee men as they stood ready for the referee's whistle was enough to create a wholesome respect for them. Kilpatrick, the curly-haired brunette from Bridgeport, started the game by kicking off to Mississippi's 25-yard line. Mississippi tried unsuccessfully to penetrate the purple line and Myers kicked to the center of the field. Kilpatrick tried to hurdle Redhead, but was stopped short. He was more successful around Foster, however, and succeeded in planting the oval ten yards on the good. The patched-up Seibels tried to pass Henry, but failed. Shortly after this Sewanee's costly fumbling appeared for the first time. Kilpatrick juggled the oval and Clapp, the Memphis lad, smothered it in neat fashion. The recovery of the ball was short lived, for it was given to Sewanee on the next line-up for Mississippi's holding.

On the next play Sewanee tried Kilpatrick with a quick dash through Redhead. Clapp brought the Bridgeport down after a 10-yard gain. Sewanee was putting forth a fierce attack and with Coach Suter yelling for them to "tear 'em up," Seibels advanced the ball 15 yards more. On the next play Redhead scented the double-pass and threw Wilson with a loss of ten yards. Kilpatrick, when called upon for an advance, took the oval long enough to juggle it in a manner that would have aroused the envy of the late Prof. Hermann. In the meantime Clapp made connection and Chandler, on the line-up, was pushed over Jones for a small gain. Harvey set the red and blue to fluttering on the sidelines by hurdling Sims for eight yards. White dropped back, only to plunge forward without an inch. On a fake kick Keyes broke through and downed Hall with a thud and incidentally a loss of ten yards. Sewanee stopped the onslaught near the middle of the field and Myers punted to Simkins on his own 45-yard line. Simkins emulated the Kilpatrick juggling act and red chrysanthemums and blue ribbon filled the air. Pat Henry fell on the oval for Mississippi. Hall then dashed around Jones for seven yards. Myers went into Keyes low and hard for a short gain, and Harvey skirted four over Sims. With but a yard and a quarter to gain and the oval on Sewanee's 25-yard line, the mountain lads took on a firm brace, securing the ball on downs.

Measurement Called For.

The distance was close and Coach Lyons advanced on the field, calling for a measurement of the distance. On the referee's ruling proved correct, and on the next line-up Umpire Mallory caught a purple-striped arm around one of the Mississippi linemen. The result was that the Oxford [adherents cheered long]... immediately threw him... five yards, Wainwright... purple line took another... and secured the oval at...

Up to this time the... prised their most ardent... play had improved and... that they were not fo... start to finish. Most of... taken place in Sewanee... thereafter were on Mississippi... teil. Seibels took ten y... rick tripped over Henry... A flap pass to Seibels net... same play on the other l... advanced Kilpatrick ten... had all along put up a... threw Seibels with a loss... line then gave Mississippi... wouldn't gain and Myers... kins, who dodged back for te... the middle of the field before C... ped him. Kilpatrick fumbled... the line-up and Harvey fell o... Chanler took a few yards aro... Myers then did the juggling a... saved it for Sewanee. Small ga... patrick and Seibels brought t... Mississippi's 35-yard line. Se... five and Kilpatrick on a fake... Foster ran ten yards over the... Hall. Seibels then added five... rick planted the ball on the... yard line. Kilpatrick then ju... several crouched Mississippia... small gain and an instant lat... for Foster to save the touch... being scored by falling on the iron...

Myers commenced the ball, kicking off to Simkins, who advanced to the 20-yard line. With the wind at their back, Sewanee commenced to punt. Simpkins' first effort placed the oval in the middle of the field. Here Sewanee's magnificent defense stood out, and Myers was again forced to punt. Seibels secured the ball for Sewanee on her 15-yard line. Kilpatrick took ten before Henry could get locked around. Sewanee kicked to the center of the field, and again Mississippi found the impenetrable line awaiting her. Myers punted for 30 yards and Seibels, fumbled, Henry falling on the ball. A close formation netted Hall a small gain, and "Fatty" White took four through center.

A beautiful trial for goal from the field presented itself, but Myers punted to Sewanee's 5-yard line. Seibels hurdled and dragged around the end for a 12-yard gain, and Kilpatrick earned four. Small gains carried the pigskin near the center, and Jones, on the fake attack at Mississippi's right flank, ran across the field, with Wilson affording good interference, for a great run of 30 yards. Seibels then set the royal purple to waving by a sensational run down the side of the gridiron for 20 more. The double pass lost ground, but Seibels skirted Henry and succeeded in getting an open field. He was finally downed by Myers. Then Seibels took a hand in the juggling act and it was Mississippi's ball on her own 25-yard line. Clapp's forward pass then gave the oval to Sewanee, and Kilpatrick was carried around Henry for ten yards. The red and blue held good and secured the ball on downs. Myers punted poorly for 15 yards. A delayed pass brought the ball to Mississippi's 15-yard line. Kilpatrick failed to gain and was brought down by Chanler. Seibels took 4 1-2, and on a fake attack at center Kilpatrick skirted Foster for the second touchdown. Sims kicked an easy goal. Score, 12 to 0.

Again did luck favor the Tennesseans. As the official timers announced that there remained but 12 seconds to play. The game was called after both teams had lined up and exchanged courtesies in the kicking line.

GAMES ELSEWHERE.

Texas Off for Vanderbilt.

AUSTIN, Tex., Nov. 14.—The University of Texas football team will leave here tomorrow to play a game at Nashville Saturday with Vanderbilt University there, and proceed to New Orleans for a game on Monday. They carry nineteen men, having materially strengthened their team during the past week.

FOOT-BALL

BILLINGS PARK. NOV. 14, 1899.

SEWANEE VS.

UNIVERSITY OF MISS.

ADMIT ONE.

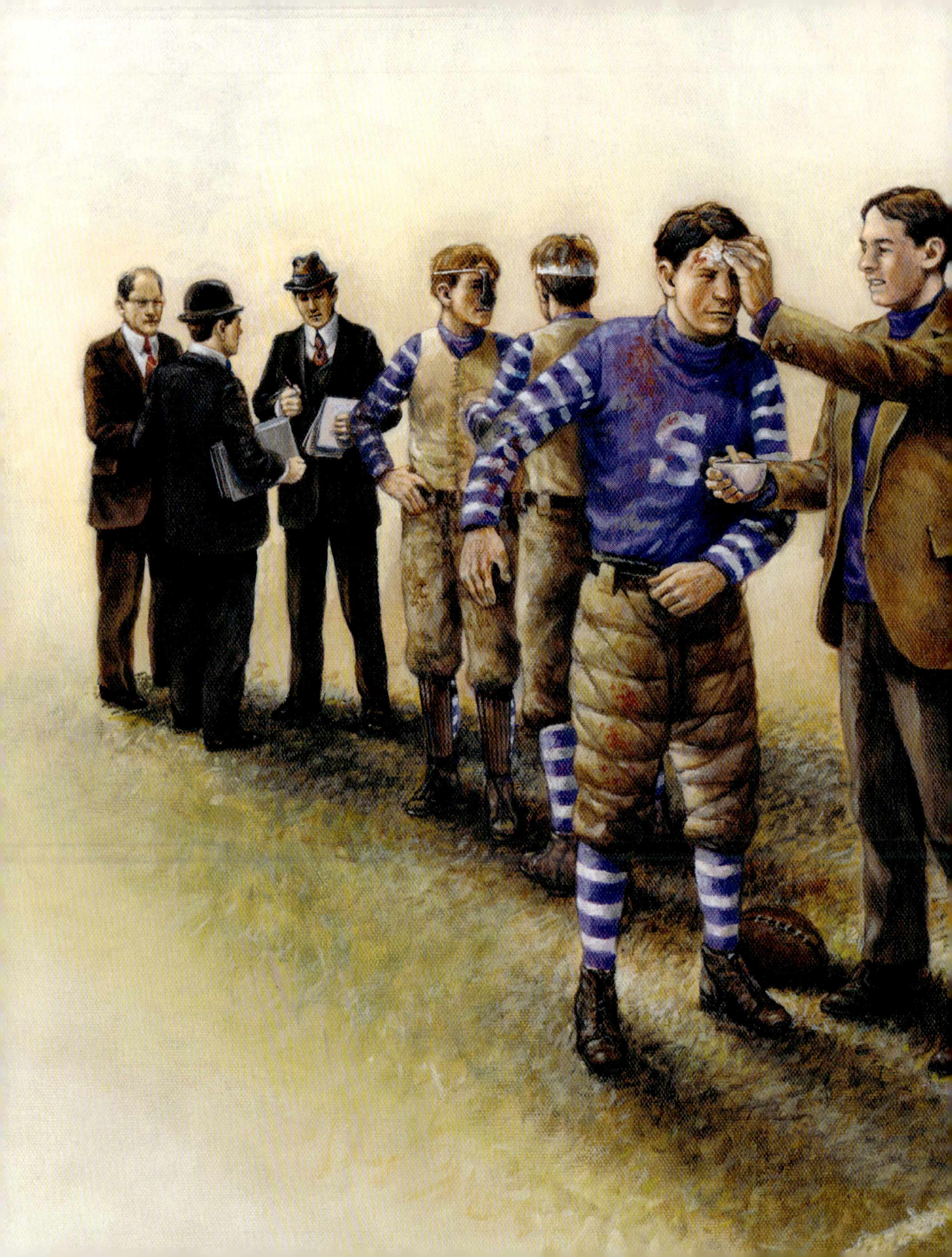

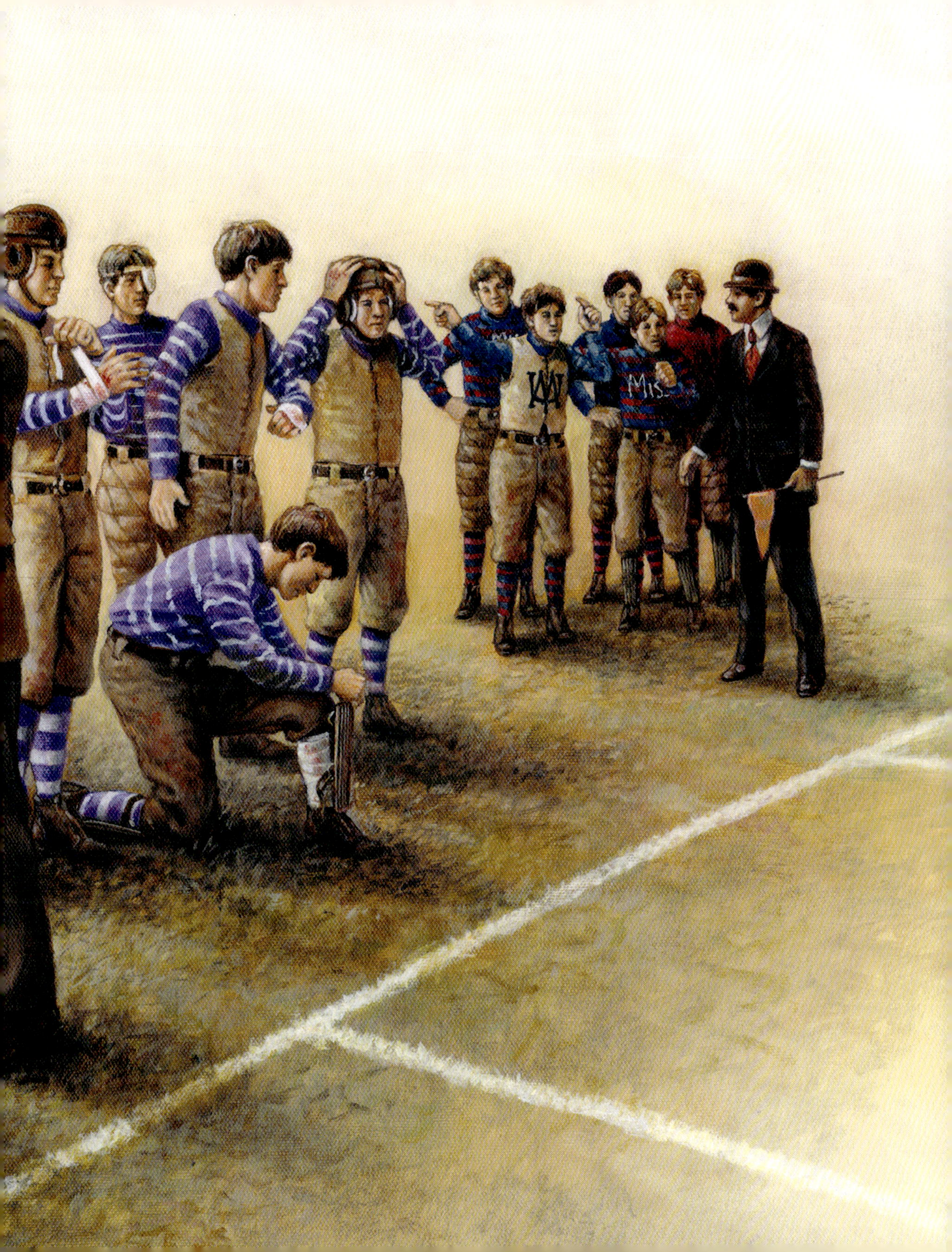

"The 1899 road trip was an incredible adventure. They had taken a beating but had won. Now, they were going onto the next one, riding across the country, trying to sleep some, looking out the windows—some of them going to places they had never seen before.

It had to be exciting. It had to be one of the greatest adventures of college students of that generation as they went from school to school to school and eventually came back to Sewanee bearing, in classical terms, the laurels of victory." —*Jerry Smith*

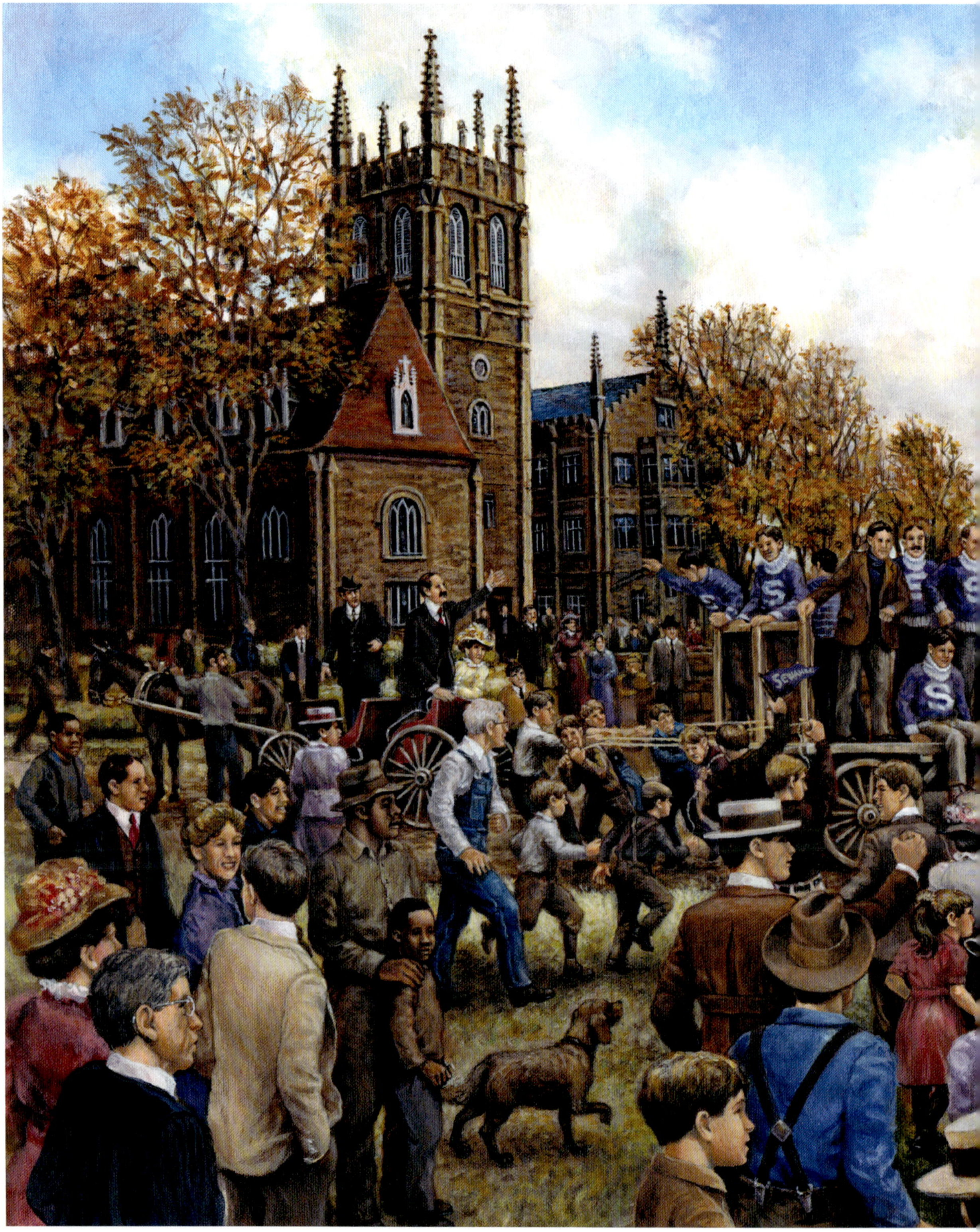

The team returned to the campus after winning all five games by a combined score of 91 to 0. They were welcomed with a huge celebration on campus.

"The young men were picked up at the Sewanee depot, put on carts, and then paraded up University Avenue to the main campus—cheered the entire way, fireworks going off, the Vice Chancellor riding in the front car. Then afterwards enormous bonfires."
—Register

Left: HOMECOMING CELEBRATION, Sewanee, Tennessee, November 15, 1899

111 | THE SEASON

TIMEOUT

A poster created about the team states that after the road trip, "On the 7th day, they rested."

While the biblical reference is poetic, it is far from accurate.

•

"The whole moniker, the Sewanee team won five games in six days, and on the seventh they rested, actually they didn't. … Today's football players would go on strike or boycott if you got back from a road trip of which you won five games in six days. They would rest for the next year. These poor guys had to go play three more games." —Savage

"People always talk about the five games in six days. What they don't remember is they played a complete schedule that year, and that six-day trip had to be incorporated into the rest of the schedule." —Barnhart

"To think of a team that can go through playing five games in six days and, instead of like, 'Hey, you made it to the finish line. Great job. Congratulations. You guys are dominant,' they just continue and play 12 games in six weeks." —Herbstreit

"There's a lot made about the five games in six days but, to me, there's not been enough made about Sewanee playing possibly the two finest teams in the South [Auburn and North Carolina] in three days." —L. Majors

Right: Poster created for U.S. Steel

In 6 days Sewanee beat Texas, Texas A&M, Tulane, LSU, and Ole Miss. On the 7th day, they rested.

Scrawny, little Sewanee. All of 300 students. Who seemed to pick the year 1899 to bellow, "We ARE the University of the South."

Sewanee won 12 games that year. All of them. They scored 322 points to 10 for the opponents. Auburn, alone, dared to score all 10. And lived to tell about it.

Like a daredevil motorcyclist, making passing runs at a suicidal leap, Sewanee took Georgia, 12-0; Georgia Tech, 32-0; Tennessee, 46-0; and Southwestern, 54-0.

Then they floorboarded it. Won 5 games in 6 days on a 2,500-mile barnstorming screamer.

They fell like this: 12-0 over Texas in Austin, Nov. 9; 10-0 over Texas A&M in Houston, Nov. 10; 23-0 over Tulane in New Orleans, Nov. 11; 34-0 over LSU in Baton Rouge, Nov. 13; 12-0 over Ole Miss in Memphis on Nov. 14.

And indeed they rested.

But that must have made them nervous. They went back home to Tennessee and took it out on Cumberland, 71-0.

1899. Maybe you didn't know football existed in the South then.

In that year 1899, when Sewanee was burning the biggies, we were tapping the first heat of steel from the new open-hearth plant at Ensley, Alabama. This was Birmingham district's first commercial steel plant. It was an historic year.

We were known as Tennessee Coal, Iron and Railroad Company then, in the South. The company moved from Tennessee to Alabama in 1886 and put together the type of mining, coking and iron manufacturing facilities it would take to finally pour steel in commercial quantities. On Thanksgiving Day, in 1899.

And on the first day of the 20th century, we made our first commercial shipment of steel. To a customer in Connecticut.

We and Sewanee were having our moment in 1899, in our own separate ways. But ironically, our histories crossed in the middle of that century.

In 1857, when the Sewanee Mining Company was about to become known as Tennessee Coal & Iron Company, U.S. Steel's predecessor in the South, we donated 10,000 acres of Tennessee mountaintop land upon which a university would be built.

And that would be The University of the South. Still known as "Sewanee" throughout the Southland.

CUMBERLAND

MONDAY, NOVEMBER 20
Hardee Field
Sewanee, Tennessee

GAME 10

In Game 10, Sewanee manhandled Cumberland 71 to 0. Bart Sims scored 11 extra points during the game, which is still a Sewanee record.

At this point in the season, Vice Chancellor Wiggins, who was a big fan of football, wrote a letter on November 28 about the season to that point: "Our foot ball team has had a most wonderfully successful season, from every point of view. … During our long trip, our boys made a reputation for clean play on the field, and for quiet, gentlemanly behavior off it, that would gratify our most fastidious friends. The team has been so well trained this year that there is not a member of it but that shows improvement in his whole bearing. We have two heavy games to play this week, and our season ends." [53]

Sewanee had played ten games in five weeks. This grueling schedule had left many players with injuries, which required Coach Suter to move players around. Incredibly, all of the players were still able to play.

Above: Cumberland team 1903 **Right:** Letter from Benjamin Wiggins to Silas McBee, November 28, 1899

114 | UNRIVALED: SEWANEE 1899

VICE-CHANCELLOR'S OFFICE
THE UNIVERSITY OF THE SOUTH.
SEWANEE, TENNESSEE.

November 28, 1899.

My dear Mr. McBee:

Your letter of 25th inst. is duly received. I cannot understand why you failed to receive the report of the dean and of the treasurer of the theological department unless it was addressed to you at Lincolnton, N.C. - the address in our printed list of the Board of Trustees furnished by the Secretary of that body. I send you another report, and trust it may reach you.

As for the way in which you can "serve the cause", there is no one who knows better how to do this than yourself, and I, therefore, refrain from making any suggestions - at least just now. When I see you in New York,—where I hope to be between this and the 10th of December - we may be able to formulate some plans together.

Our foot ball team has had a most wonderfully successful season, from every point of view. While the individual players have not been so good as we have had in some years, yet the coach has taught them how to play together, and the result is that today they have piled up 311 points to opponents' nothing. The men are not laid out after a play; the men on the other side are, though. During our long trip our boys made a reputation for clean play on the field, and for quiet, gentlemanly behavior off it, that would gratify our most fastidious friends. The team has been so well trained this year that there is not a member of it but that shows improvement in his whole bearing. We have two heavy games to play this week, and our season ends. I wish you could be down here to see these games, for I know you would enjoy them quite as much as any of us.

With warmest regards, I am,

Yours very sincerely,

B.L. Wiggins
Vice-Chancellor.

115 | THE SEASON

AUBURN

THURSDAY, NOVEMBER 30
Riverside Park
Montgomery, Alabama

GAME 11

Sewanee's next opponent was Auburn, coached by John Heisman.

"John Heisman was supremely confident, sometimes bordering on an arrogant man. Everybody understood that. He built programs at Clemson, built a program at Auburn, built a program at Georgia Tech. We all remember Georgia Tech beating Cumberland only 222-0. At halftime it was 146 to nothing, and John Heisman said, 'You know, you're going to have to play harder in the second half because you just can't trust those guys from Cumberland.' " —Barnhart

The Auburn game was scheduled to be played on Thanksgiving Day in Montgomery. The Sewanee team had a terrible train ride to Montgomery and arrived late. Many years later, Ditty Seibels wrote Luke Lea about the game, stating, "Did we not arrive in Montgomery quite late without having had breakfast? It was a very unsatisfactory game from start to finish. I believe you acted as one of the linemen and were pretty well pummeled before you got back to the hotel. My brother Temple and other members of the family were mixed up in the free-for-all fight." [54]

Ralph Black later recounted an incident that occurred before the game: "Manager Luke Lea of Sewanee stationed himself in the tiny ticket booth at the entrance of the field. After the crowd, including ladies in carriages and lassies on horseback, had entered the field, Manager Lea call [sic] for a division of the receipts. The Auburn manager … preferred to delay the pay-off. After some argument, Manager Lea pulled a pistol and announced immediate division of receipts. Gun in hand, he counted out dollar for dollar." [55]

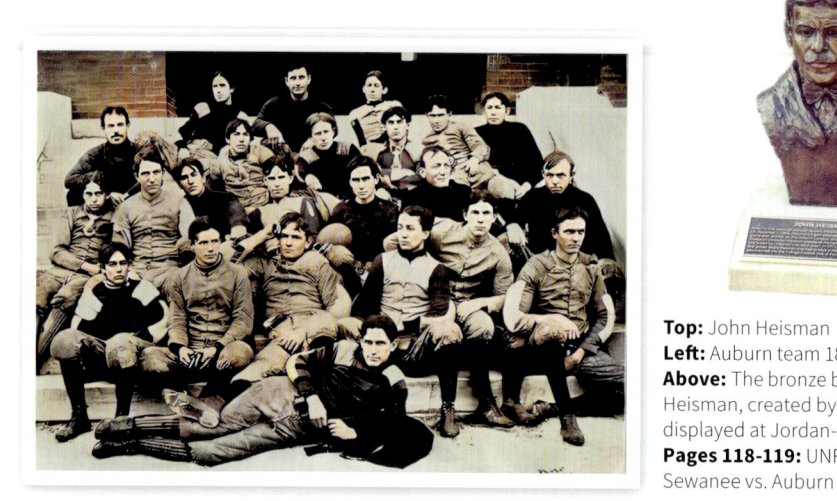

Top: John Heisman
Left: Auburn team 1899
Above: The bronze bust of John W. Heisman, created by Ken Bjorge, displayed at Jordan-Hare Stadium
Pages 118-119: UNRULY CROWD, Sewanee vs. Auburn

THE AGE-HERALD, FRIDAY, DECEMBER 1, 1899

THE PLUCKY AUBURN TIGERS GO DOWN IN DEFEAT BEFORE THE PURPLE-CLAD LADS FROM SEWANEE

A SUPERBLY FOUGHT GAME

The Purple Had Advantage in Weight, But Auburn's Work Was Fast.

Montgomery, November 30.—(Special).—After two hours of fierce fighting over the tricky pigskin, the football giants from Sewanee snatched a well-earned victory from the plucky Auburn lads this afternoon and won the southern championship by the slim margin of one point.

It was a bitterly fought battle from beginning to end, and though each team made two touch downs, the Orange and Blue failed to land one goal, and the game went to the Tennesseans by the score of 11 to 10.

Four thousand gaily bedecked spectators had assembled to witness the contest and on every side the purple and the orange and blue floated in the slight breeze which was blowing across the field.

Sewanee clearly had the advantage in weight, but the swift work of the Auburn ends and backs, together with several tricky plays, made up the deficiency, and it was a case of see-saw throughout both halves.

Auburn made the first touchdown and prospects were indeed bright for the orange and blue. Before time had been called, however, Sewanee had duplicated the play and had the ball back of Auburn's goal line, tieing the score.

It was a battle for blood in the next half, but both teams again succeeded in making touchdowns. Auburn was unfortunate in being unable to send the ball between the purple's goal posts, and the score stood 11 to 10 in favor of the Tennesseans.

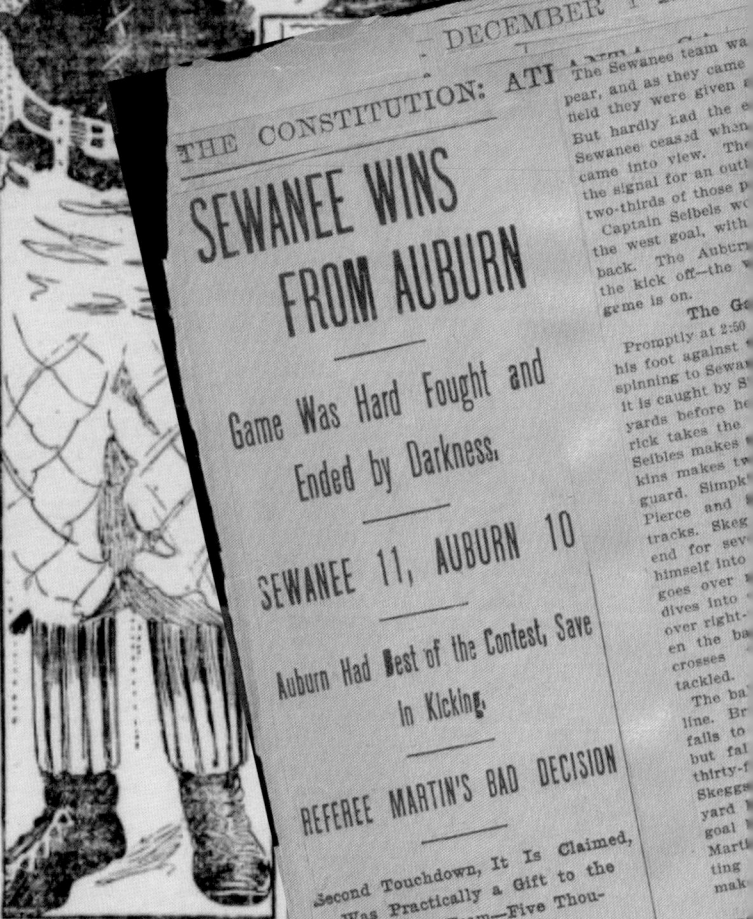

EVENTFUL JOURNEY

Yacht Zeba Arrives at Pensacola After a Trip of 6,007 Miles

Pensacola, Fla., November 30.—The naphtha yacht Zeba of New Orleans, 32 feet long

---

DECEMBER 1 1899

THE CONSTITUTION: ATL

SEWANEE WINS FROM AUBURN

Game Was Hard Fought and Ended by Darkness.

SEWANEE 11, AUBURN 10

Auburn Had Best of the Contest, Save In Kicking.

REFEREE MARTIN'S BAD DECISION

Second Touchdown, It Is Claimed, Was Practically a Gift to the Sewanee Team—Five Thousand Spectators Saw the Game.

By W. R. Tichenor

The Sewanee team wa pear, and as they came field they were given But hardly had the Sewanee ceased when came into view. The the signal for an out two-thirds of those p Captain Seibels wo the west goal, with back. The Auburn the kick off—the w game is on.

The Ge

Promptly at 2:50 his foot against spinning to Sewan it is caught by S yards before he rick takes the Seibels makes kins makes tw guard. Simpk Pierce and tracks. Skeg end for sev himself into goes over dives into over right en the ba crosses tackled.

The ba line. Br falls to but fal thirty-f Skegg yard goal Mart ting mak

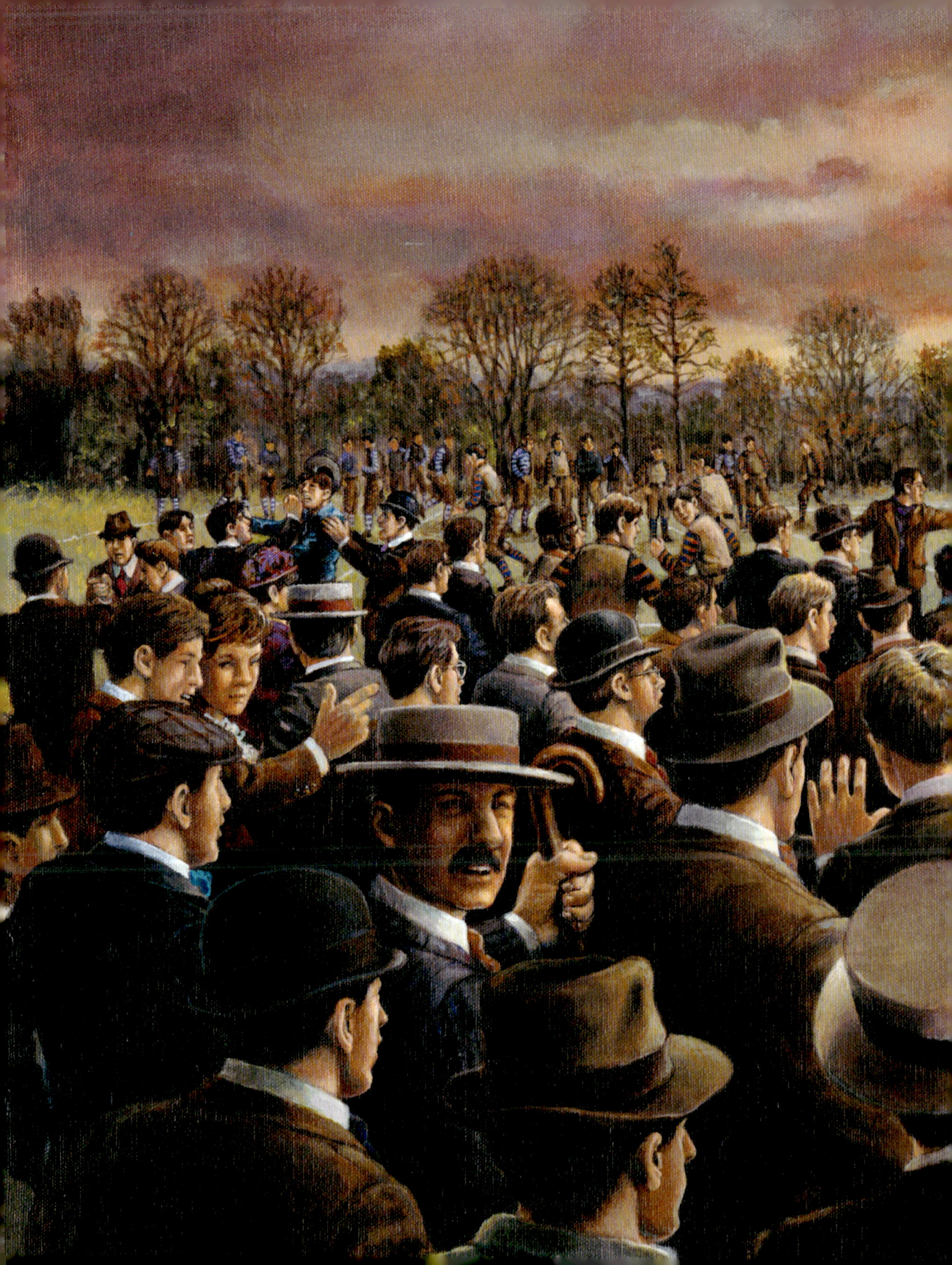

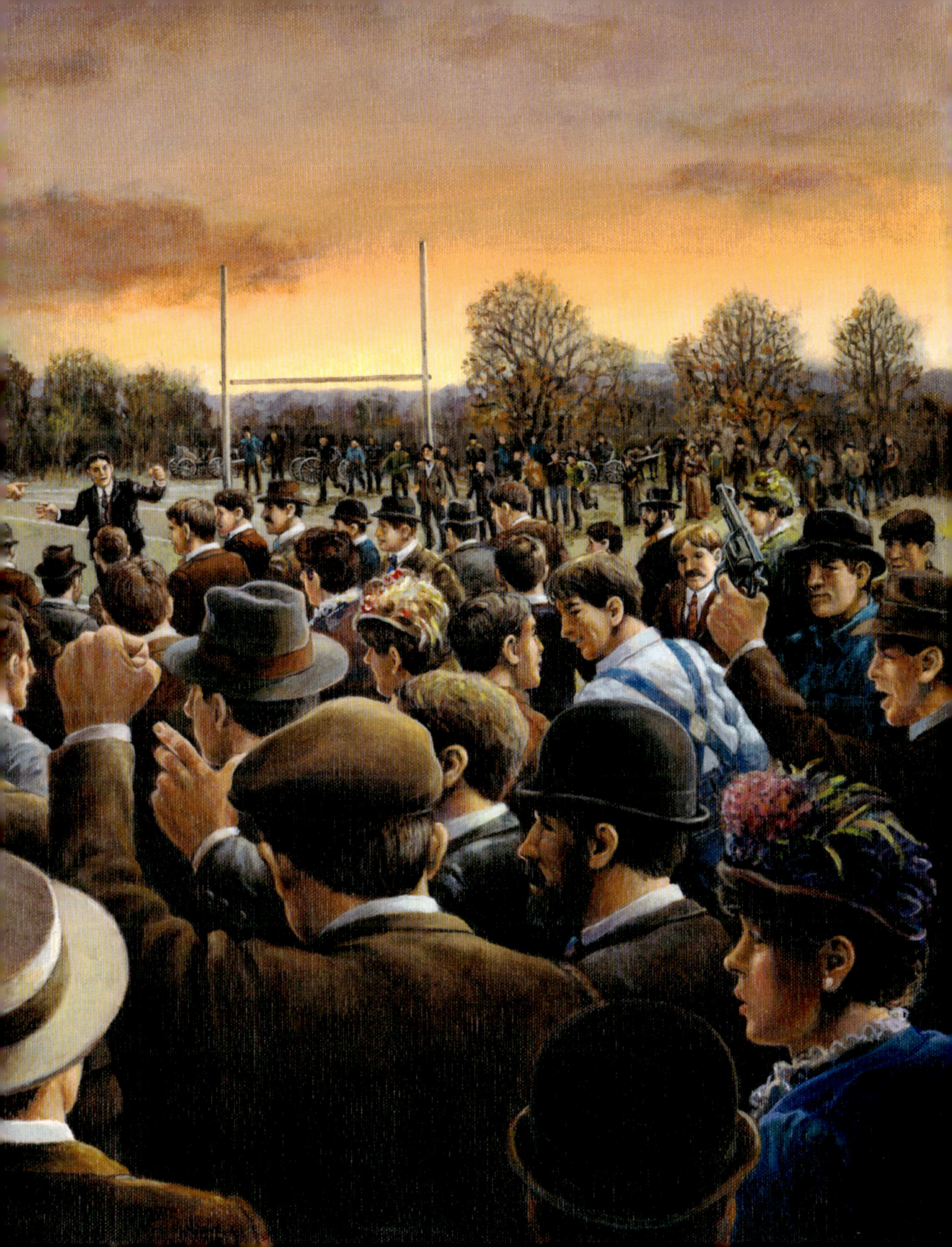

This was a rough game from start to finish and has been described by Coach Vince Dooley as "almost a riot, kind of a barroom brawl." A crowd of 4,000 showed up for the game.

After the game started, Sewanee discovered that Auburn had sewed leather handles on their pants so that players could grab the handles and pull a runner forward or the runner could grab the handles of players in front of him. They would also lock arms to form an illegal wedge, and this tactic was killing Sewanee. At one point, Suter told his players to run at this formation as fast as they could and lead with their cleats up to hit the legs of the lead interference.

Coach Suter complained about the handles and, at one point, the referee stopped the game and required Auburn to cut the handles off the pants, which incensed Heisman.

Lea wrote Seibels in 1943: "You will recall that at one time Taylor, the referee, cut handles off the belt of the Auburn players to the number of seventeen. This game was played before the days of stadiums and the spectators and substitutes lined up on the sidelines. At one time seventeen Auburn players were counted in an Auburn offensive play, six substitutes feeling they had an opportunity for service." [56]

Warbler Wilson wrote: "The [Auburn] substitutes were placed along the side lines and kept coming into the interference. We were playing outside the City limits, no police protection and the large crowd kept closing in when the game was stopped by Woods [the referee] because the teams didn't have a 100 feet square to play in." [57] There were a number of disputed calls by the referee, and all of these interruptions delayed the game.

This was a hard-fought game, and Auburn was getting the better of Sewanee. They were the first team to score on Sewanee this season, and at halftime the score was Sewanee 11, Auburn 10.

The lore of the Seibels family is that at halftime, Emmet Seibels came down to his brother and said, "Ditty, you've got to do something. We bet the house on the game. We'll lose the house. We'll have to kick your mother out." —H. Seibels

In the second half, Auburn was threatening to score and perhaps win the game when the referees called the game for darkness after only 14 minutes had elapsed. The Auburn fans and Coach Heisman were outraged and claimed that they had been cheated. At the end of the game, Auburn had rushed for 323 yards to Sewanee's 82.

"My great granddaddy … received some sort of blow to his abdomen that had a lifetime effect on his digestive system. So it had to be a pretty severe blow to do that. He didn't come out of the game. He said it was definitely the roughest game they had played during the whole season." —Faircloth

"I think all great football teams or maybe all great sports teams in general need a lot of luck. That was the day they were luckiest. … Suter and Lea took the win and left town as quick as they could and headed to Atlanta." —Register

Luke Lea in a letter to Ditty Seibels in 1943 said about the Auburn game: "Phelan Beale saved my life that day. I acted as lineman in the second half and an Auburn supporter was about to hit me over the head with the other lineman's stick when Phelan drew his gun. Thereupon there was the largest number of guns I ever saw drawn until I was in the Meuse-Argonne [in World War I]." [58]

Above: Lea, Seibels, and Suter **Right:** Correspondence between Seibels and Lea; letter from Black to Seibels

JEMISON-SEIBELS
INSURANCE
BIRMINGHAM, ALA.

March 12, 1943

Honorable Luke Lea,
Nashville, Tennessee.

Dear Luke:

My memory does not serve me well enough to recall except vaguely why our '99 Team did not measure up to its vaunted reputation in the game with Auburn in Montgomery on Thanksgiving Day 1899, and which we won by a score of 11 to 10. I lost my football scrapbook and must rely upon my memory for our failure to put up a better fight. Did we not arrive in Montgomery quite late without having had breakfast?

It was a very unsatisfactory game from start to finish. Auburn accused Referee Williams (?) of Virginia of having thrown the game to us and it wound up in a nasty row. I believe you acted as one of the linesmen and were pretty well pummeled before you got back to the hotel. My brother Temple and other members of the family were mixed up in the free-for-all fight.

Of course I know that we had just finished our famous Texas trip from which we had not recovered, but if we had had a decent night's rest we would have made a better showing.

How we hated Auburn in those days! Years later I came to know a lot of Auburn alumni and actually made a substantial contribution to Auburn's support. It is a splendid institution of its kind.

Do you recall taking up Heisman on a $250.00 bet that North Carolina would beat Sewanee in Atlanta on the following Saturday?

If you have THE PURPLE giving an account of this game I would very much appreciate your sending it to me.

When you have time, let me know if I recall correctly what occurred.

With best wishes,

Sincerely yours,

H. G. Seibels

HGS-j

Heisman + I got to be good friends even before I left Sewanee. He was a brilliant coach

---

808 OAKDALE ROAD, N.E.
ATLANTA, GA.

Aug. 25, 1949.

Dear Ditty;

Here's my rambling answer to yours of 22nd., and I remember that only 16 players went on the Texas trip-add Suter and Luke Lea with our negro rubber makes up the list. In addition to the regulars were me, Lee KirbySmith,Bish.Colmore, Dan Hull and Harris Cope. Thats how I make out the list.

Dont you remember our breakfast at Texarkana, where the train stopped for time out, the stories of the street shootings across the State line which was down the center of the main St,,where Sheriffs could not cross to make arrest- the fancy calls of the restaurant man- Ham and eggs etc. Keep em Red eyed- Slap em once etc. After this we wrolled into Dallas beat the Univ. of Texas. The Sewanee folks and us so happy and hilarious over our victory, the fine dance beautifull Texzas Gals. the curfew at ten off to Houston in our Tourist sleeper etc. the care to drink only out of our Tremlet Spring water barrel. Texass A and M a bigger battle than Texas then on to New Orleans- Rest on Sunday,?? trip on Lake Charles,Snipe Dinner etc. Tulane and La. easy, then on over night train to Memphis where we had an awfull tiresome game with Miss. The Miss.Capt wanted to have the Referee make us take off those hard leather helmets,not he fair etc. they had none. We kicked till us ends were tired too-well do I remember Poola trying to pick me up in the back field. Why dont you go for a touchdown, that was after i had dived on the ball on fumble by their back after I tackled him. Field open but me I did exactly as coach Suter said dive on that ball and dont loose it etc.

The Auburn game as you know was won in the 2nd. half- They had us 10 to 6- by a complete change of tactics- Suter had Dan Hull,Harris Cope and me on the side lines off to our selves to watch closely for their criss crosses etc. and make up a defense. We gave them the Kick Quick Split Bucks,stopped their plays and won. How General Wood saved us with his fearless refereeing etc. Then the trip to Atlanta when Coach Heiserman sore on being beat etc. flashed a $100.00 bet that we would not beat NC. then you will know haow we empty our pockets of dimes and dollars to cover every cent he had. How we had fun over this for we knew we would win etc. The Big Dance my aunt Mrs. Joseph Thompson gave the team at the fashioable OLD BALL Room at the Kimball House here in Atlanta. That NC. game awfull kicking game, the NC half the jumping Kohler from the professional Orange NJ. club- We fooled him for we raised up and downed him on his jumps. How we held NC for 9 downs inside our ten yd. line and then that marvelous place kick by Kil from the 36 yd. line for a drop Kick for Goal the only score. We saw no more of Heiserman but enjoyed spending his money on riertorious living in Atlants.

Kindly excuse my typing but I know that the party writing the story will Dress it off right. I did this writing myself and am asking that you have your Secreatary rewrite it after your perusal etc. Am in hurry to get this off by Air Mail so heres best of luck to you and come to see me. Rgards to all, Come to Atlanta Sept. 8th. for our Sewanee Dinner ask Chitty about this.

Ralph.F.Black.

Washington, D. C.
April 7, 1943.

Mr. H. G. Siebels
c/o Jemison-Siebels Inc.
Birmingham, Ala.

Dear "Ditty":

It was fine to hear from you again, and your letter of the 12th was received while I was on a prolonged absence from Nashville and forwarded to me here.

Your alibis are no good. While I have no data at hand my recollection was that the close score was due to three causes. First, the team had an off day caused probably by its previous strenuous schedule and by what so frequently happens, a team being good one day and bad the next. Second, Auburn was out to win the game in any way possible. You will recall that at one time Taylor, the referee, cut handles off the belt of the Auburn players to the number of seventeen. This game was played before the days of stadiums and the spectators and substitutes lined up on the sidelines. At one time seventeen Auburn players were counted in an Auburn offensive play, six substitutes feeling they had an opportunity for service.

There were three great disputes in the game. One when Dan Hull caught his own free kick. This happened twice and both times raised a storm when the referee permitted Sewanee to hold the ball. The second was when we were about to lose the ball on downs and the end instead of the middle of the ball was over the required five yards gain for first down. The third was when the referee after holding Auburn offside on an attempted kick for goal allowed a second attempt but penalized Auburn ten yards. Auburn missed the goal.

Heisman threatened not to put his team on the field the second half unless the referee reversed himself and would have adhered to that decision had I not informed him that the contract provided for the forfeiture of the half of the gate receipts to the team that left the field before the end of the game for any cause and his salary was in the gate receipts then reposing in my name in the safe at the Exchange Hotel.

Auburn was so bitter that the score was contested before the SIAA in Atlanta that December. I represented Sewanee and Auburn lost as I recall it. It was a vote of 18 to 3.

Phelan Beale saved my life that day. I acted as lineman in the second half and an Auburn supporter was about to hit me over the head with the other lineman's stick when Phelan drew his gun. Thereupon there was the largest number of guns I ever saw drawn until I was in the Meuse-Argonne.

I have no copy of the Purple and cannot recall whether I had a scrapbook of the game or not.

I remember a bet with Heisman but do not recall the amount.

With warmest personal regards, I am

Very sincerely yours,

Luke Lea.

Above: A FLYING WEDGE, Sewanee vs. Auburn

122 | UNRIVALED: SEWANEE 1899

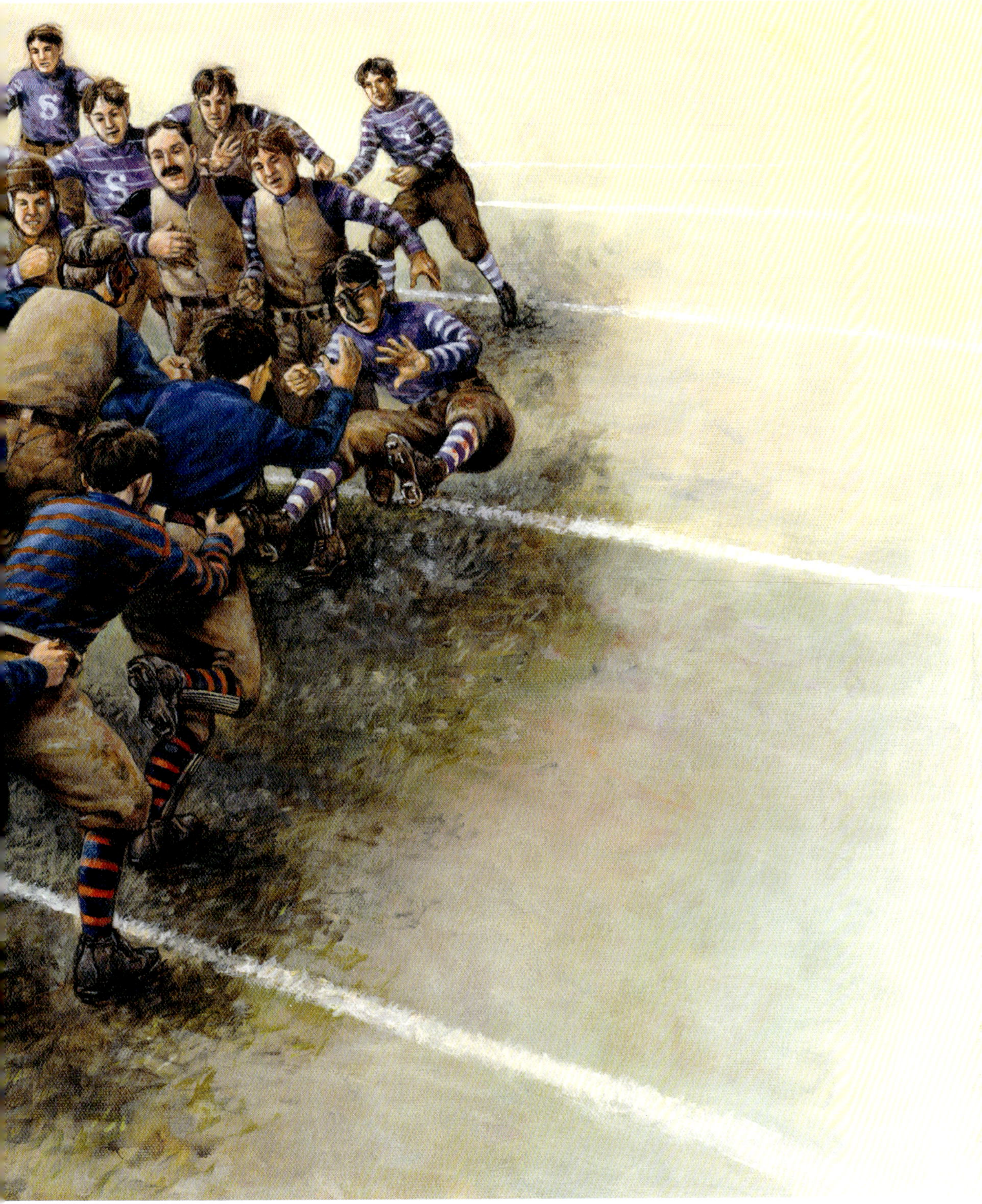

TIMEOUT

Raging Battle

"I've heard that fights in hotel lobbies for years after that game could be started by anyone taking a strong position on either side of the argument."

On December 13, 1899, Squire Brown wrote in the SPORTING NEWS: "It would be an extremely difficult proposition to determine which was the hardest fight—the Auburn-Sewanee football game here on Thanksgiving Day or the aftermath of that battle, an aftermath that has been raging ever since." [59]

After the game, Heisman was so upset that he threw fuel on the fire of controversy when he wrote THE BIRMINGHAM AGE-HERALD newspaper, which published his letter on December 4, 1899. In part, Heisman stated, "I think we completely outplayed Sewanee from start to finish, both offensively and defensively. I think the work of both officials was, by all odds, the worst I ever saw, and I don't mind proclaiming it from the house tops." [60]

Interestingly, Umpire Taylor responded to Heisman's letter with his own letter to the newspaper published on December 6, 1899. Taylor replied, "I have read with amused interest the rabid communication of Mr. J. W. Heisman in today's issue of the Age Herald. This professional coach, would-be 'actor of character parts' (to quote his own words to me), expert gambler in football futures, and would-be professor of elocution and oratory, considers the sporting world out of joint and that he, like Hamlet, is 'born to set it right.' To those who know Mr. Heisman, his loud mouthed utterances have little weight and his assertion that he was 'dragged' into this discussion can only provoke a smile." Taylor critiqued Heisman as someone with "histrionic gifts," making "lurid appeals," and seeking "peanut gallery applause" for "heroically acted character parts" in some "cheap theater." [61] Heisman even responded to Taylor's letter.

In 1954, Arthur Ben Chitty at Sewanee wrote to an editor for SPORTS ILLUSTRATED about the Sewanee-Auburn game of 1899, saying, "I've heard that fights in hotel lobbies for years after that game could be started by anyone taking a strong position on either side of the argument." [62]

TIMEOUT

The Montgomery Advertiser (Montgomery, Alabama) · 13 Dec 1899, Wed · Page 8

SPORTING NEWS.

SQUIRE BROWN.

It would be an extremely difficult proposition to determine which was the hardest fight—the Auburn-Sewanee football game here on Thanksgiving Day or the aftermath of that battle, an aftermath that has been raging ever since.

Birmingham Age Herald 12-6-1899

THE AGE-HERALD, MONDAY, DECEMBER 4, 899.

COACH HEISMAN SCORES OFFICIALS

Discusses at Length the Sewanee-Auburn Game.

HE HAS BEEN MISQUOTED

The Celebrated Trainer Says That Auburn Clearly Outplayed Sewanee at Every Point But Got the Worst of All Decisions.

Coach J. W. Heisman of the Auburn football team and an ex-member of the University of Pennsylvania team, is in the city. Mr. Heisman is considered one of the best football experts in the United States and talks very interestingly of the

UMPIRE TAYLOR ANSWERS HEISMAN

Says Auburn Team Was Poorly Coached.

WANTS CLEAN ATHLETICS

Suggests That if the Auburn Trainer Has More to Say He Should Present it to the Southern Intercollegiate Association.

THE AGE-HERALD, FRIDAY, DECEMBER 8, 1899

HIESMAN MAKES REPLY TO TAYLOR

Says the Umpire's Answer No Argument.

THAT AUBURN IS WITH HIM

The Coach Writes That Instead of Admitting Error, That Mr. Taylor Attacks His Reputation As An Actor

"won except for that decision——" and here an argument just 37 years old broke out again between the two old-time coaches—an argument I still recall from that far-away, long-ago period of foot ball—before even Fielding H. Yost had gained any national fame.

Both Suter and Heisman still remembered every detail of the play in question—and still disagreed.

In 1935, Grantland Rice for the EVENING STAR in Washington, D.C., interviewed Suter and Heisman. They discussed a disputed call by the referee, and the reporter noted, "Both Suter and Heisman remembered every detail of the play in question—and still disagreed." [63]

125 | THE SEASON

NORTH CAROLINA

SATURDAY, DECEMBER 2
Piedmont Park
Atlanta, Georgia

GAME 12

The final game of the season was scheduled for December 2 in Atlanta. Ironically, one of the North Carolina coaches was J.G. "Lady" Jayne, who had been the Sewanee coach the year before and who had recommended Coach Suter to take his place at Sewanee. North Carolina's head coach was Billy Reynolds, who had also previously coached at Sewanee.

"Heisman made a bet, apparently, against Sewanee when they played North Carolina. Somebody told all the players and that got them really fired up to play as well as they could against Carolina, not just to win that game but to give Mr. Heisman a second disappointment." —Prunty

Ralph Black added to the story: "You will know haow [sic] we emptyd [sic] our pockets of dimes and dollars to cover every cent he had." [64]

North Carolina also played on Thanksgiving Day, beating Georgia by a score of 5 to 0. Although at that time it was considered unethical to scout your opponent, Sewanee players were tipped off by some Georgia players that North Carolina had a back named Koehler who would leap over his players near the goal line to score. Sewanee thus prepared itself to meet the leaping Koehler and stop him. Koehler was also a tramp or ringer athlete, because he was actually a semi-professional athletic club player, not a full-time student.

Left, top: J.G. "Lady" Jayne **Left, bottom:** North Carolina team in 1899 **Above:** THE SEWANEE PURPLE, December 14, 1899; THE ATLANTA CONSTITUTION, December 3, 1899

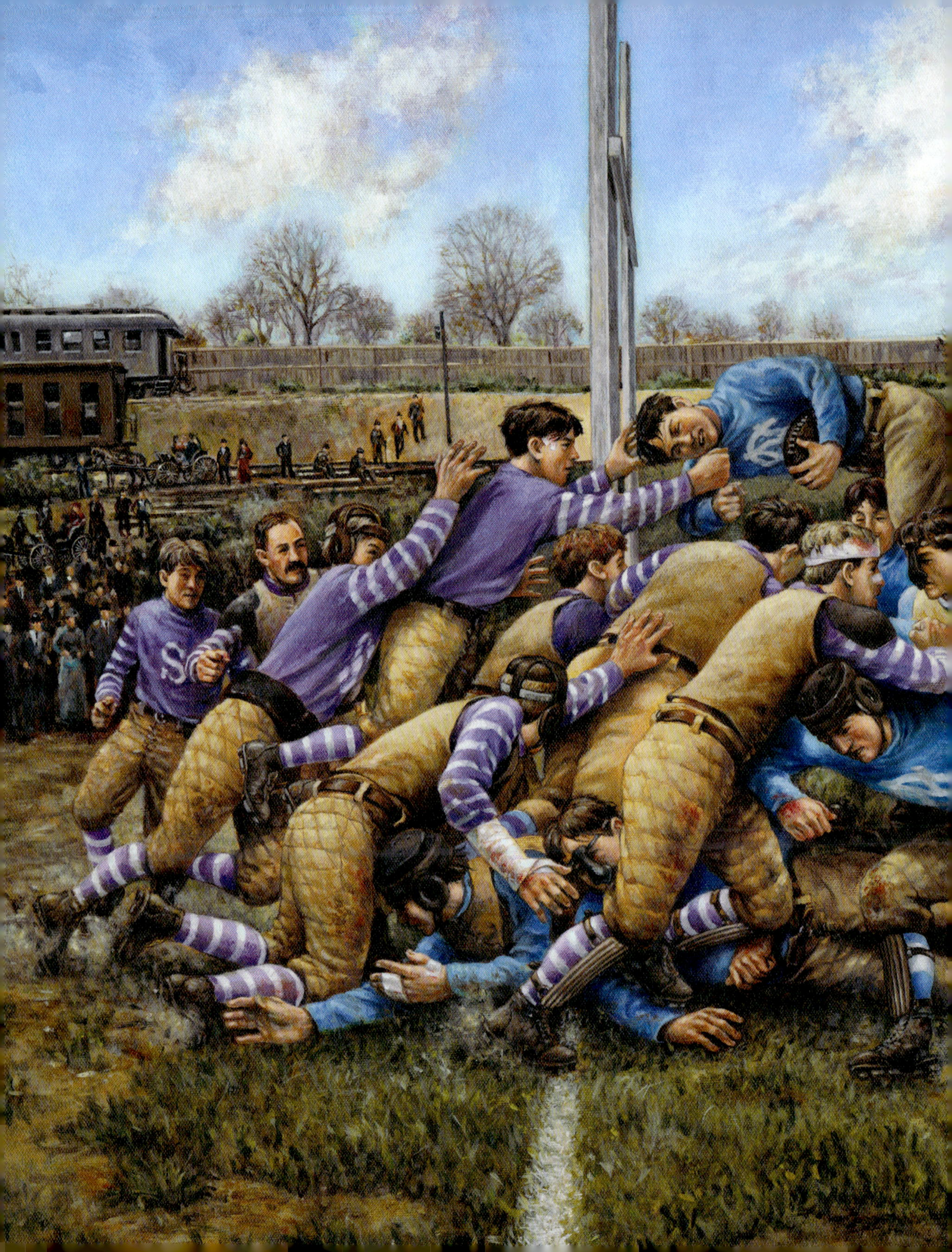

Sewanee's undefeated season looked to be in jeopardy. There were 43 punts in the game, and it was a very close contest. At one point, North Carolina had first down on Sewanee's one-yard line. They had five attempts to score because Sewanee was penalized twice for offsides. Sewanee was prepared for Koehler, however, and stopped him from scoring. The Sewanee yearbook in 1900 gave its version of this goal line stand: "Koehler is called on again, he rushed fiercely against that adamantine wall, hangs poised above the goal-line one second, and Captain Seibels twists him back before he has breath to say 'down.' The strain is over and Sewanee gets the ball within three inches of defeat." [65]

Left: GOAL LINE STAND, Sewanee vs. North Carolina

"When you lose in a close game, the first people you point to are not yourselves. You point to calls that were missed, penalties that were unjust. You point to this pattern of cosmic injustice."

—WOODY REGISTER

Later in the game was another pivotal moment. Warbler Wilson later described this critical play: "In the second half of this game, I was playing the backfield, as I always did, and North Carolina kicked—it was a high spiral. I signaled for a fair catch on the 42nd yard line and was tackled, which gave us 15 yards and the choice of play. We were about ten yards from the sideline. I called Kilpatrick and held the place kick. He kicked it six or eight feet above the cross bars." [66]

"My grandfather, the last game of the season against North Carolina, kicked a field goal, which was five points at the time, to win the game."
—Rex Bray

A final element of drama occurred when the referee called the game at 30 minutes, instead of 35 minutes, just as North Carolina was threatening to score. The North Carolina fans were very upset by this call, as well as by Suter's coaching from the sidelines.

"You get a different version of that championship game depending on the sources you read. There really are no neutral sources. The Atlanta newspapers give you one account. The Sewanee newspapers give you another. Those in North Carolina give you a strikingly different account. … When you lose in a close game, the first people you point to are not yourselves. You point to calls that were missed, penalties that were unjust. You point to this pattern of cosmic injustice." —Register ■

"A Fair Catch."

Above: CAP AND GOWN 1900

131 | THE SEASON

Above: KILPATRICK'S WINNING FIELD GOAL, Sewanee vs. North Carolina

133 | THE SEASON

FOOTBALL NUMBER
The Sewanee Purple

VOLUME XIV.　　　UNIVERSITY OF THE SOUTH, DECEMBER 14, 1899.　　　VOLUME XIV.

CHAMPIONS OF THE SOUTH.

CHAMPIONS OF THE SOUTH

Sewanee 11　Auburn . . 10
Sewanee 5　North Carolina 0

THE THANKSGIVING GAME.

The Thanksgiving game of '99 has become history, but there are many details which will ever be fresh in the minds of those who witnessed the contest.

Sewanee reached Montgomery Thursday noon, after a hard night's travel, and after a light lunch donned the football uniforms and were driven out to the field. The men were worn out and had none of the ginger which has characterized all of the Sewanee games this season. Nevertheless, every one went into the game with a determination to do or die, and but for the many foul tactics employed by the Auburn team, the score would undoubtedly have been different, and Sewanee would have finished the season with an uncrossed goal line. Auburn's interference was foul, and the conduct of some of the spectators was fouler. Affidavits can be secured from reliable persons that on more than one occasion an Auburn substitute would leave the side lines and run in the interference. Sewanee has never before played an opponent who used such un-sportsmanlike methods, and if the feelings of future teams are given the least consideration, she will hereafter meet only those teams who regard the ethics of football.

The officials were powerless to act, as they thought that a decision, however just, which would penalize Auburn for foul interference, would inaugurate a row, and leave the contest unfinished. So, rather than render such a decision, which would result in the contest becoming a draw, they allowed the game to proceed until darkness interfered and put an end to the most disagreeable contest ever played on a Southern gridiron.

The second half was never finished, as the crowd would surge on the field and the officials would have to suspend play and try to keep them behind the ropes. On one occasion the Sewanee linesman found it necessary to speak with the referee regarding the unfairness of Auburn's linesman. In his eagerness to reach that official he broke the line and started on the field. The Auburn man, without the slightest provocation, attempted to strike him, and had not cooler heads prevailed, a general row would have ensued.

Again, when Wilson scored the second touch-down and the ball had been down some ten seconds, an Auburn player deliberately jumped upon him, and but for the intervention of outsiders, blows would have been exchanged.

On another occasion, while near the side lines, and during a scrimmage, a Sewanee player was kicked by a spectator who, jackal like, sneaked away to boast of his cowardly deed.

These are but a few evidences of the happenings on Thanksgiving Day, and are mentioned to show the public the things we had to contend with while in Montgomery.

But the game is over, and despite the fact that Mr. Heisman has made the broad statement that Auburn outplayed Sewanee, and can do it any day in the week, we have the satisfaction of knowing that on Thanksgiving Day in the last week of November, we defeated his team, and no matter how prolific his statements, the score will stand.

The following is clipped from the *Montgomery Advertiser* of December 1st:

"Comparisons are said to be odious. Perhaps the troublesome things are, but a bit of one right here will not be very much out of place.

"Mr. Heisman brought his team in Wednesday night; they had a good night's rest that night, and arose greatly refreshed on Thursday morning. They have played four games this season, not having to go over one hundred miles for either game. Yester-

(Continued on second page.)

CHAPTER 8

Champions of the South

"The story might read like an epic poem, if it had not become prosy to us through dent of repetition, but the world must know, and those yet unborn must know what mighty things Sewanee can do and has done, and so they are writ here." —The Sewanee Purple [67]

The team was welcomed back in Sewanee with a joyful celebration. For the season, Sewanee had scored a total of 322 points to their opponents' 10. As noted in the yearbook for that year, "The night of the '99 football demonstration, when we had won the championship for the South, is an illuminated page in Sewanee's history. You could have read a newspaper out at Morgan Steep by the glare of the bonfires." [68]

It was already clear to everyone at this point that Sewanee's amazing season was indeed historic. Not only had they gone undefeated in 12 games, but their five games in six days was already mythic.

"At the end of the season, people on campus and observers who were writing in newspapers … saw this as a team for the ages—that it was a monumental achievement." —Register

Suter later went on to work for Luke Lea, who was the owner of the *Tennessean* newspaper in Nashville. Suter hired a new reporter named Grantland Rice. In a 1944 interview with Rice, Suter reflected on his team's accomplishments: "We had three major football assets … First, we had the finest football spirit that any football team has ever shown. Can you imagine a squad today playing five games in six days, and a player kicking when removed for rest? Second, we had stamina and fibre, the ability to take more punishment than any of our rivals could give us, and hand it back. Third, we had football skill—especially kickers, tacklers, and ball carriers." [69]

Ditty Seibels had his own reflections on the success of the team. In a radio talk the night before the 1931 Sewanee-Auburn game, he observed: "To what was Sewanee's brilliant success due? I attribute it to one thing alone, and it is the greatest thing any team can have, teamwork. There was about the team an esprit de corps that was truly wonderful. Like the three musketeers, their motto was 'One for all and all for one.' Discipline was perfect. There were no jealousies, only the indomitable will to win, that unconquerable never-say-die Sewanee spirit." [70]

"You speak of intangibles of individuals, but then as a team you speak of the intangibles of a team playing together with this great camaraderie." —Dooley

"The key is the word team—team, team, team. The number one thing is loyalty and togetherness." —Bowden ■

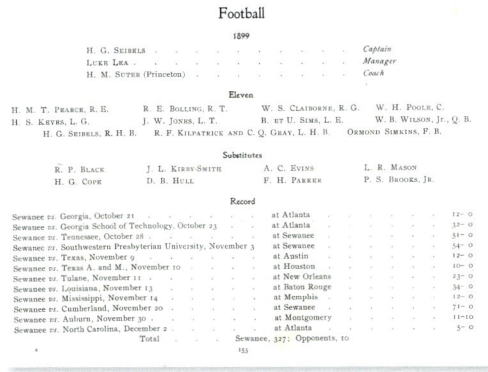

Left: THE SEWANEE PURPLE special football edition **Above:** CAP AND GOWN 1900, page 157

OFFICIAL RECORD OF TEAM

Sewanee vs Georgia, October 21	at Atlanta	12 – 0
Sewanee vs Ga. School of Technology, Oct. 23	at Atlanta	32 – 0
Sewanee vs Tennessee, October 28	at Sewanee	46 – 0
Sewanee vs Southwestern Presbyterian Univ., Nov. 3	at Sewanee	54 – 0
Sewanee vs Texas, November 9	at Austin	12 – 0
Sewanee vs Texas A. & M., November 10	at Houston	10 – 0
Sewanee vs Tulane, November 11	at New Orleans	23 – 0
Sewanee vs Louisiana, November 13	at Baton Rouge	34 – 0
Sewanee vs Mississippi, November 14	at Memphis	12 – 0
Sewanee vs Cumberland, November 20	at Sewanee	71 – 0
Sewanee vs Auburn, November 30	at Montgomery	11 – 10
Sewanee vs North Carolina, December 2	at Atlanta	5 – 0

Total – Sewanee 327
Opponents 10

The first two games of the season were played at Atlanta, one on Saturday, October 21st, against Georgia and the other on Monday, October 23rd, against Georgia Tech, Sewanee winning 12 to 0 and 32 to 0 respectively. Five days later we played the University of Tennessee at Sewanee and won 46 to 0. Then followed the famous Texas trip on which we travelled over 2500 miles, played 5 games in 6 days against very strong teams. Texas was much the best team. Sewanee won all five games. Only six days later Sewanee beat Cumberland University 71 to 0.

We left Sewanee with a squad of 18 players, Manager Luke Lea, Coach Suter and a Negro rubber. We traveled in an old tourist car and carried our own water. Luke Lea gave us a dinner Monday night and we arrived in Dallas in good shape, Tuesday afternoon. We played Texas on Thursday, attendance about 7500. We won 12 to 0. I suffered a fractured rib and a bad gash above my eye and still bear evidence of the scar. The game against Texas A & M was comparatively easy for us but we were tired after an all night ride and won only 10 to 0. The next day (Saturday) was the easiest game of all, Tulane never got within 25 yards of our goal except on the kick-off. L. S. U. at Baton Rouge on Monday and University of Mississippi at Memphis on Tuesday were comparatively easy games but we were tired out when we played the University of Mississippi otherwise the score would have been much larger. Mississippi was a weak team. When in New Orleans we were given a theatre party at the Tulane Theatre and James K. Hackett, the star of the play, wore our colors and made complimentary reference about the team.

Only six days after we returned from the Texas trip we had to play Cumberland University and piled up our largest score and probably Sewanee's largest score against any opponent – 71 to 0. Ten days later we played Auburn in Montgomery. After an all night ride and a late breakfast (the train was several hours late) we tackled Auburn (A.P.I.). We won 11 to 10, the game breaking up in a row. Heisman was Auburn's coach and he went with us to Atlanta where he had agreed to play the University of North Carolina on Saturday for the championship of the South. North Carolina had beat the University of Virginia and the University of Virginia had beat Vanderbilt. Heisman bet $250.00 on N. C. We won 5 to 0. As you probably know this game was played in two halves of 30 minutes each. North Carolina had the ball within one foot of our goal during the second half and could not put it over in three downs. We scored on a field goal from about the 40-yard line.

It may be seen from the above that Sewanee played 12 games during the season, the first two in 3 days, and the next two within eleven days, then five in six days and the last two in three days. In other words, ten of the twelve games played during the season, four were played in six days and five in six days. This is truly a remarkable record and will probably never be equaled. Alonzo Stagg published the record in the Saturday Evening Post many years ago, Grantland Rice has referred to it in numerous articles and seldom a year passes I do not receive some newspaper account of this famous football team.

Above and right: Henry G. "Ditty" Seibels' later recollections about 1899 season from the Seibels' family files

SEWANEE'S 1899 FOOTBALL TEAM

The regulars on the squad were as follows:

R. F. KILPATRICK, L. H. B. — A fast hard runner and fine on interference. (I think he is a realtor in New York City)

H. G. SEIBELS, R. H. B.

ORMOND SIMKINS, Fullback — (Deceased) The best defensive player of his time and a beautiful back. He and I played in the backfield when on defensive. We passed laterally and very effectively. This was before the days of the forward pass. Of course we passed backward.

BARTLETT ET ULTIMUS SIMS, L. E. — Better than average End. (Killed in an automobile accident 7 or 8 years ago)

W. H. POOLE, Center — (Theological student---deceased) The best Center among the Southern football teams.

R. W. "Pap" BOLLING, R. T. — (Deceased) A tough Texan and a fierce tackler-- a good defensive player.

J. W. JONES, L. T. — (Theologue---deceased. Had few equals and no superior as a tackle.

W. S. "Bish" CLAIBORNE, R. G. — (Deceased) A great fighter as he was later a Minister.

H. S. KEYES, L. G. — (Deceased) I remember very little about Dr. Keyes but I should say he was the average Guard.

W. B. "Warbler" WILSON, JR. Q.B. — Now an Attorney in Rock Hill, S.C.

R. Peters Black, R. E. — (Now Professor of Engineering at Georgia Tech) Good on both offensive and defensive.

H. M. T. PEARCE, R. E. (SUB) — (Deceased) Chaplin in the Navy. A fine End for his size - about 140 lbs.

DAN B. HULL, Fullback (SUB) — (Now lives in Savannah, Ga.) We used him on quick kicks and he was tops at it. Quick kicks were then new to the game and worked well for us.

J. L. KIRBY-SMITH (SUB) — (Deceased) Son of the famous Confederate General Kirby-Smith and a scrapper like his elder brothers who played football at Sewanee in prior years.

C. Q. GRAY (SUB)
F. H. PARKER (SUB)
HARRIS G. COPE (SUB)
P. S. BROOKS, JR. (SUB)

H. M. SUTER, COACH — (of Princeton) Sewanee never had a better Coach or one better liked. Was Managing Editor of the Tennesseean of Nashville.

LUKE LEA, MANAGER — You probably know the story of Luke Lea. Colonel Lea was probably one of the most colorful characters Tennessee ever had.

KILPATRICK   WILSON   SEIBELS   SIMKINS

CHAPTER 9

Glory and Sacrifice

"They had to play through pain, play through injuries, and play through exhaustion. They were able to do it, and that's the reason they got that name of the Iron Men. It wasn't because they were iron and they weren't hurt—they just played through it." —Robert Miller

What the team accomplished was indeed amazing; yet, there is more to the story. This is not only a saga of glory and achievement but also a testimonial of pain and sacrifice.[71]

The most poignant example was the star fullback, punter, and vicious tackler Ormond Simkins. Later in life, he suffered mightily in his legs, which had been heavily damaged playing football. His knees and legs were so badly injured that he had to have one of his legs amputated.

In 1916, Simkins wrote his teammate Claiborne, "I am no sore head. God knows I have had enough to be sore about; I have had enough to lose all my love and patriotism for Sewanee. When I think of being crippled for life I cannot help but feel bitter towards Suter and Luke Lea who insisted on my playing while I was in a crippled condition. Being crippled for life is no small matter. However, I am glad I went to Sewanee; I am proud of being a Sewanee man... Sincerely your friend, Simp."[72]

When he was 42 years old, Simkins went back into the hospital to have his second leg amputated, and he died on the operating table at Georgetown University Hospital on December 4, 1921.

"Ormond Simkins was as brave a man as ever lived. He didn't have a drop of yellow blood in him, ever. And he was one of the greatest football players who ever lived."[73]

Although Simkin's teammates may not have exhibited this level of severe injury, it is clear that many of them suffered various ailments related to football for the rest of their lives. The team's motto, "No-body Hurt," is inspiring but not realistic given the violence of the game. ∎

"Being crippled for life is no small matter."
—SIMKINS

Left: SEWANEE'S FOUR HORSEMEN **Above:** Ormond Simkins

ORMOND SIMKINS
ATTORNEY AND COUNSELOR

2nd. May 1916.

My Dear Claiborne:-It has been some little time since I answered your last letter. Please forgive my remissness. I have been at Corsicana in the practice of law and have been so busy I have had little time to give to my personal correspondence.

I received an item in the Philadelphia Inquirer on the "Master Mind in Football" written by a fellow named Adler. It is just an encomium on Cope and I suppose Adler is impressed with my opinion of him else I would never have received it. It is really a very stupid opinion of Adler. My contention is that Cope is a very inefficient coach. I don't think he ever had "BRAINS". I don't think he teaches brains. Adler's idea, just like yours, is warped with prejudices. I have seen Sewanee operate under his coaching and I do not hesitate to say that Cope's coaching has been stupid and inefficient. Now I think your Sewanee men are responsible for it all; I think you Sewanee men lose games just because you cling to your prejudices. As for myself, I don't think I ever care to see Sewanee boys play like children in a football game and so I stayed away last year from Houston, Texas.

I am no sore head. God knows I have had enough to be sore about; I have had enough to lose all my love and patriotism for Sewanee. When I think of being crippled for life I cannot help but feel bitter towards Sutor and Luke Lea who insisted on my playing while I was in a crippled condition. Being crippled for life is no small matter. However, I am glad I went to Sewanee; I am proud of being a Sewanee man.

Write to me "Clay" and lets quit talking about Cope. I think he is a good fellow and a splendid influence, indeed,

Above and right: Ormond Simkins' letter to William Claiborne, May 2, 1916

ORMOND SIMKINS
ATTORNEY AND COUNSELOR

I like him better as a good man than as a coach. He sticks in my gizzard as a coach.

Please write me all the Sewanee news. If you have a Purple please send it to me. I get hungry for Sewanee news. Bishop Knight was at Dallas three weeks ago. I see they put me on that committee to raise some money for Sewanee. I am rather glad they did appoint me. If there is anything Sewanee needs it is money.

Why don't Seibles and the rest of them get busy? Some of these fellows talk so much one would think they were doing wonders. Please let me know when Commencement takes place. I may come to Sewanee for that event.

Sincerely your friend,

"Pinck"

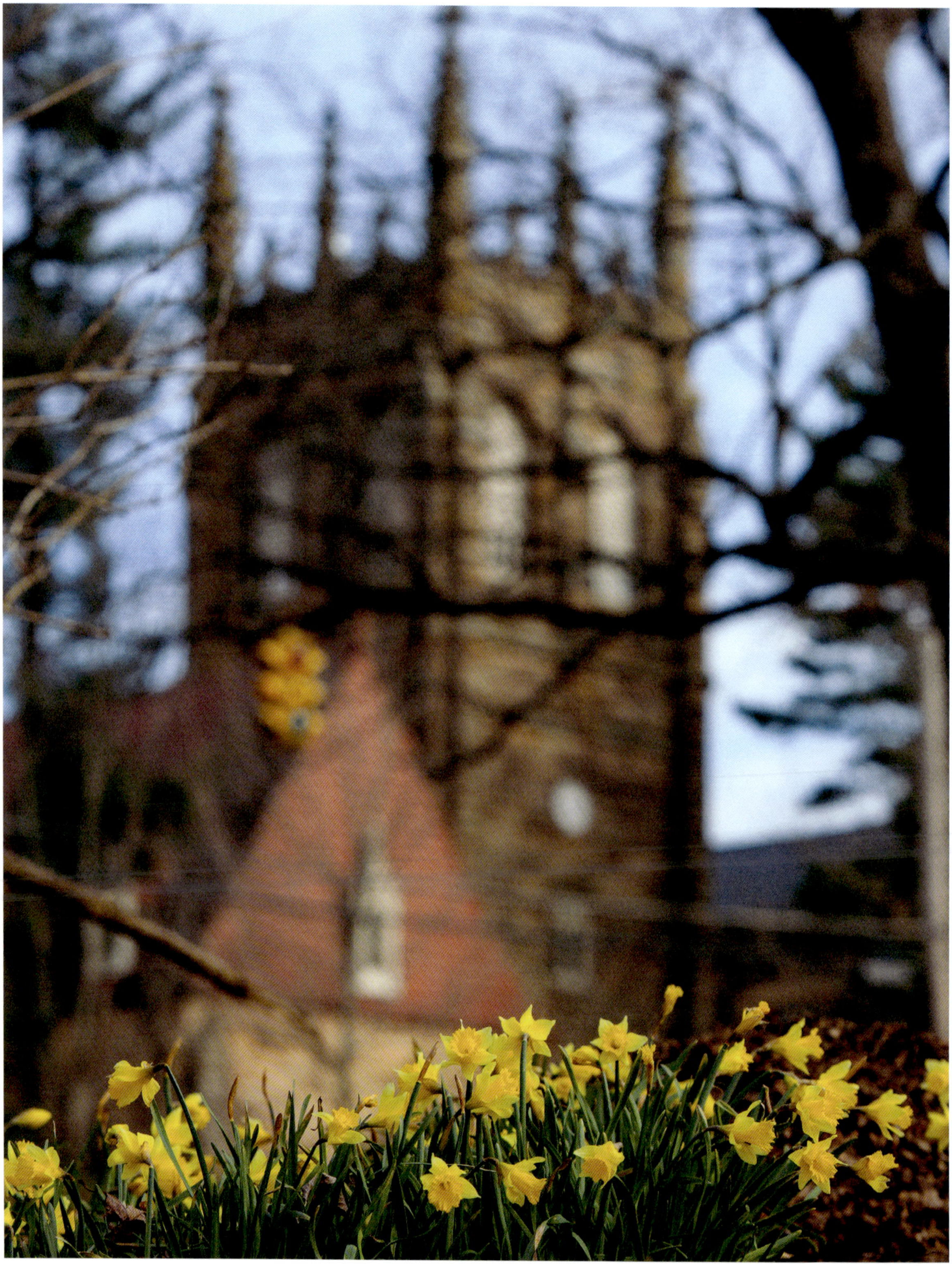

CHAPTER 10

Sewanee Today

"It's a long way away . . . in the middle of woods, on top of a bastion of mountains crenelated with blue coves. It is so beautiful that people who have once been there always, one way or another, come back. For such as can detect green apple in an evening sky, it is Arcadia—not the one that never used to be, but the one that many people always live in; only this one can be shared." —William Alexander Percy, Lanterns on the Levee

The University of the South is a residential liberal arts college offering an education that combines serious intellectual pursuit, collaborative learning, civic engagement, and spiritual growth in an unmatched outdoor setting. Established by the Episcopal Church, it is owned by 27 Dioceses of the Episcopal Church, although it welcomes students of all faiths or no faith. The University also has an Episcopal School of Theology, which trains the next generation of priests, as well as offering many opportunities to clergy and laypersons to deepen their faith. Sewanee's 13,000-acre campus on Tennessee's Cumberland Plateau provides space for study, reflection, and recreation. Largely forested and rich in biodiversity, the domain is a distinctive asset offering an unparalleled outdoor laboratory and boundless recreational opportunities. With about 1,700 undergraduates, Sewanee remains purposefully small and dedicated to building a sense of community. Almost all students live on campus all four years and share a main dining hall, which promotes a true sense of community. Sewanee is known for close faculty-student interaction and for its traditions of honor, community, and respect.

Students have administered Sewanee's Honor Code for more than 100 years, and all entering freshmen sign the Honor Code. Professors wear academic gowns to teach and there is a student Order of the Gown as well. Sewanee is committed to a rigorous academic curriculum that focuses on the liberal arts and sciences. It offers more than 30 majors and 40 minors, as well as pre-professional programs including business, medicine, and law education. The University of the South is consistently ranked among the top tier of national liberal arts universities; it has produced 27 Rhodes Scholars, 53 Watson Fellows, 34 NCAA Postgraduate Scholars, and dozens of Fulbright Scholars. The University is known as a crossroads where many of America's best writers gather; contemporary poets, novelists, and playwrights conduct writing classes, readings, and workshops as part of the Tennessee Williams writers-in-residence program. Undergraduate research thrives in areas from chemistry to economics to the visual arts, which is featured each spring in a campus-wide celebration of student scholarship and creativity. Sewanee currently has 24 varsity sports, as well as club and intramural sports, and offers a wide range of extracurricular activities and programs. ■

Left: Breslin Tower in spring **Inset:** University Seal in All Saints' Chapel

Above: Fall colors at The University of the South

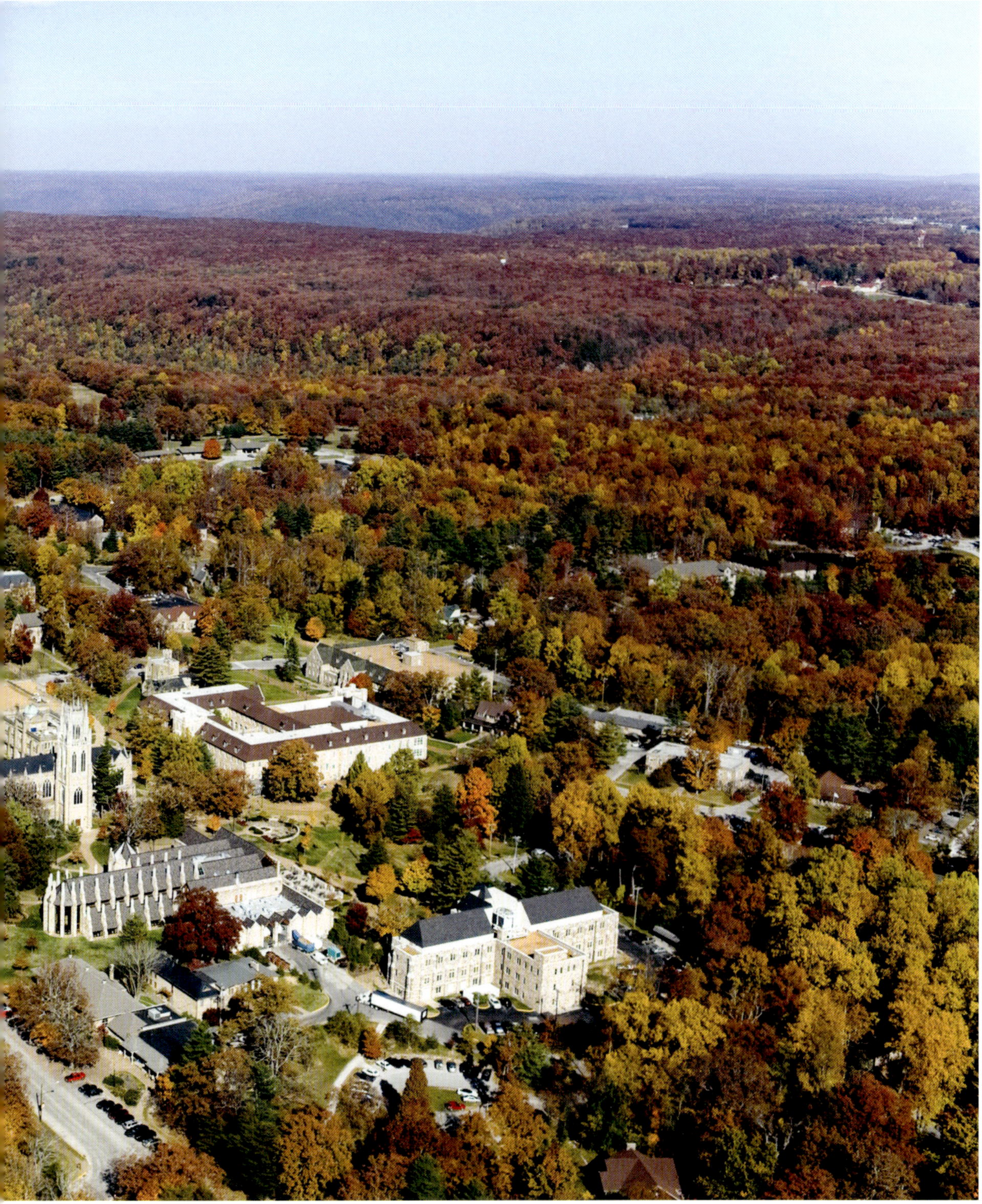

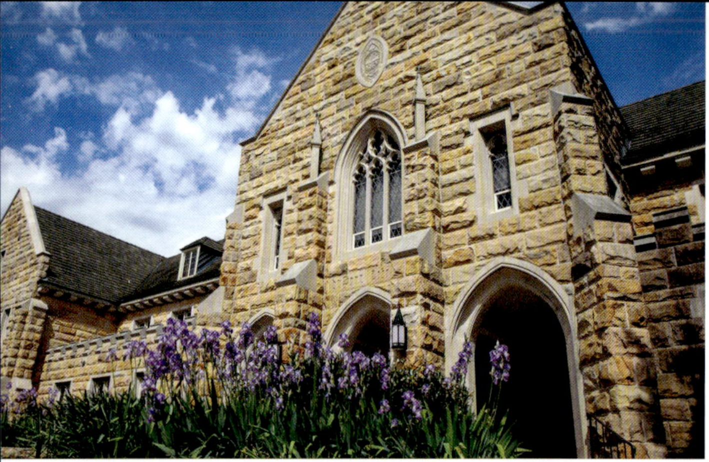
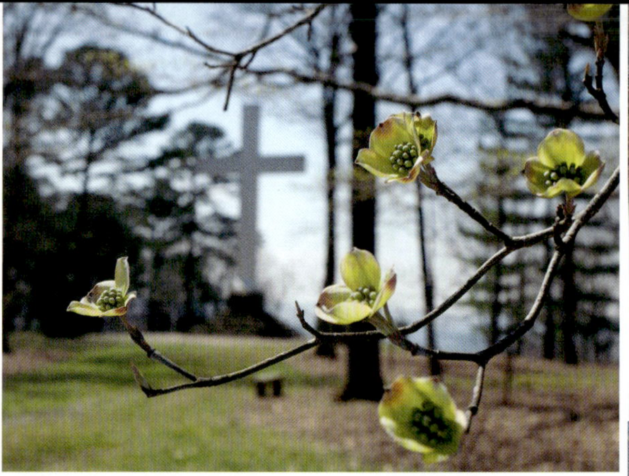
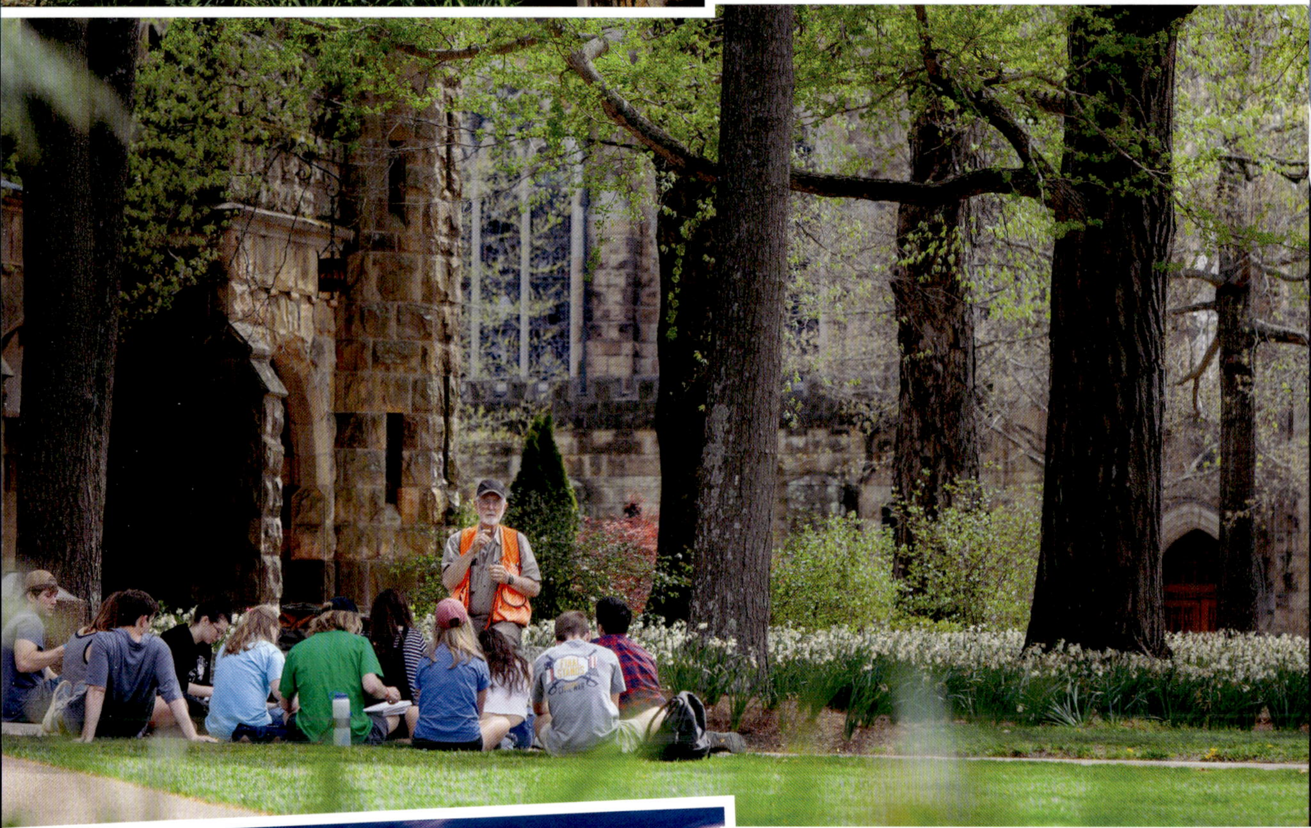
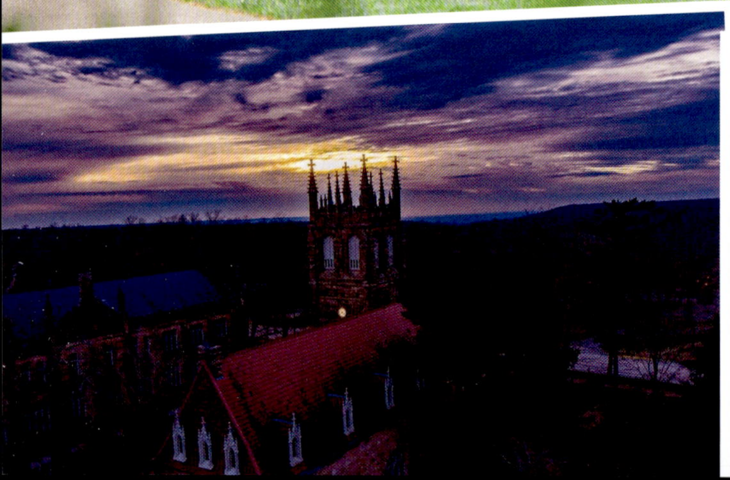
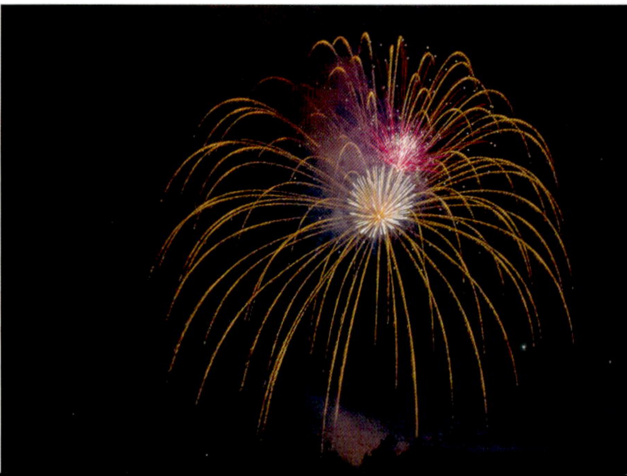

147 | SEWANEE TODAY

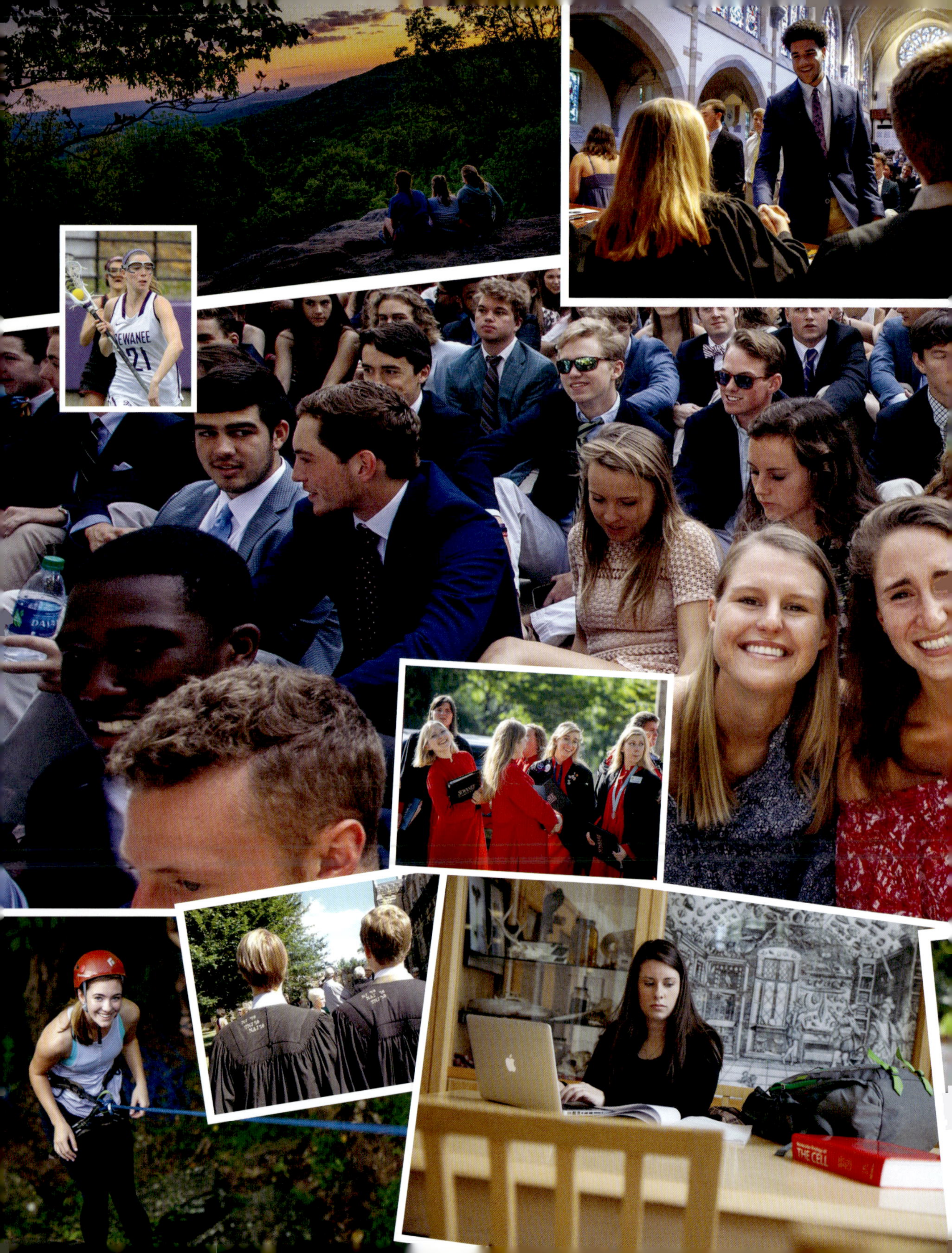
21
THE CELL

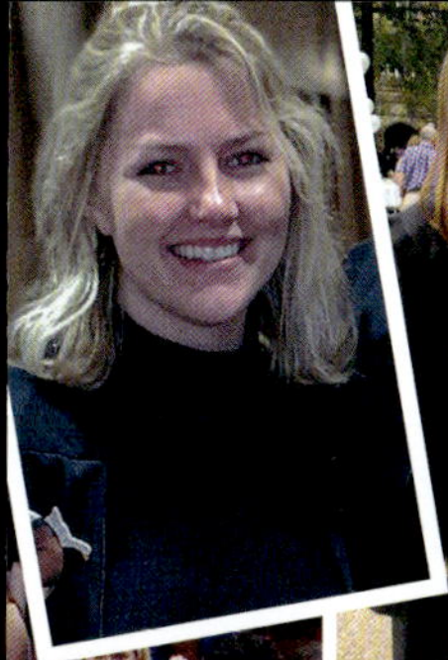
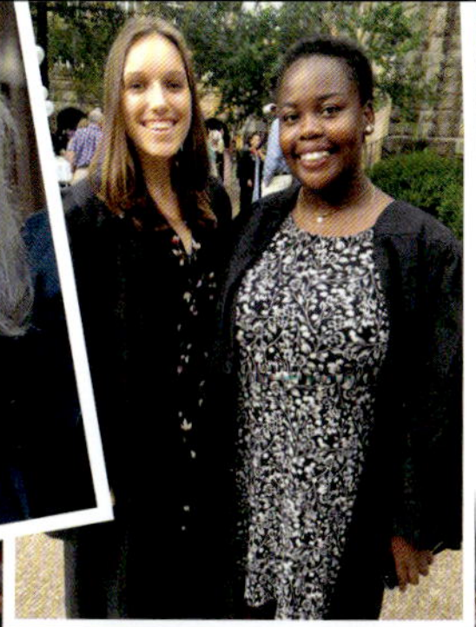
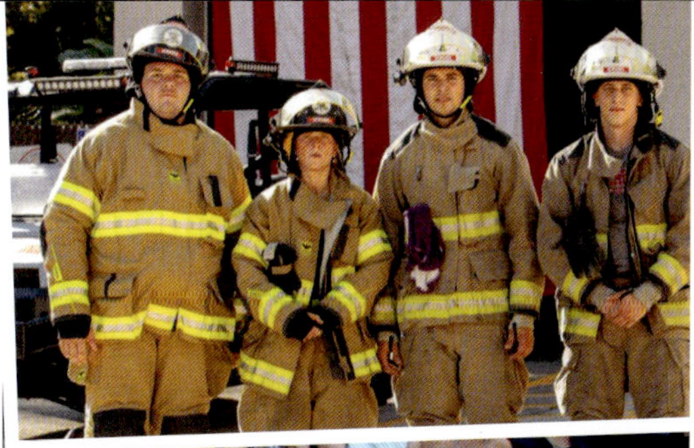
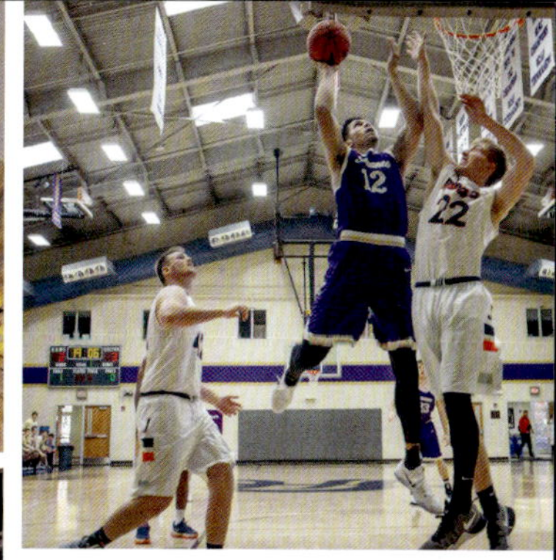
12
22
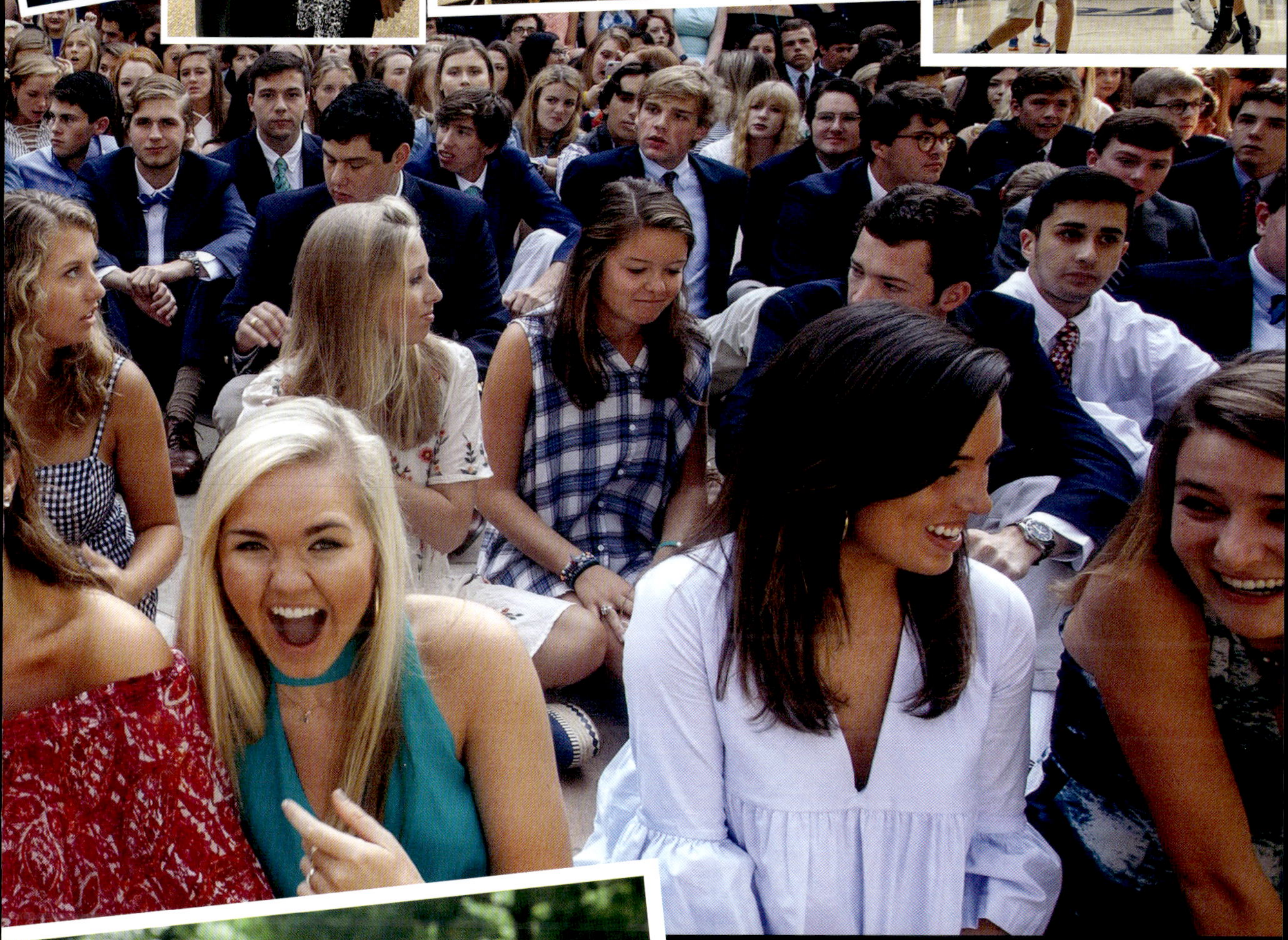
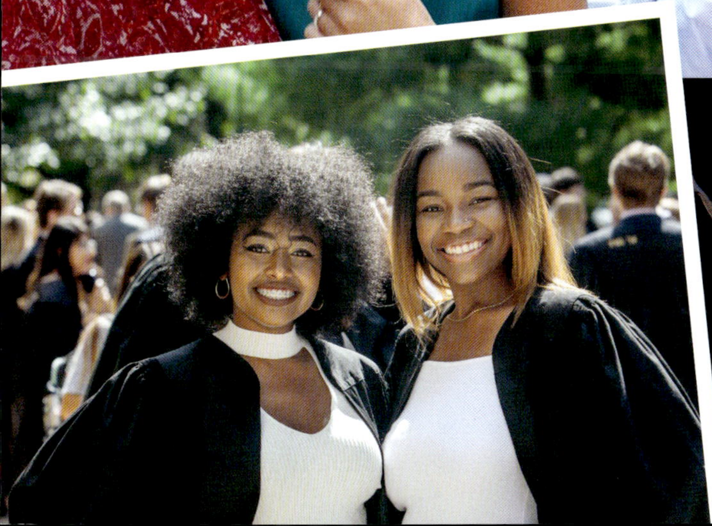
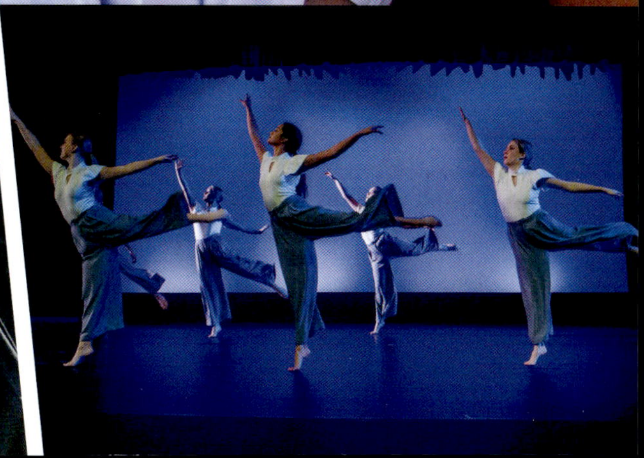

TEAM OF 1899
UNDEFEATED AND UNTIED

WON 5 GAMES IN 6 DAYS
ON A 2,000 MILE TRIP

OPPONENTS
GEORGIA, GEORGIA TECH,
TENNESSEE, SOUTHWESTERN,
TEXAS, TEXAS A & M,
TULANE, L.S.U., MISSISSIPPI,
CUMBERLAND, AUBURN, NORTH CAROLINA.

CHAMPIONS OF THE SOUTH

CHAPTER 11

1899 Remembered

"It's so amazing that we continue to be awed by it and to some great degree inspired by it. ... The institution is a strong, ongoing place, and after we're all gone from it and after the next generation comes, it's such a strong part of our legacy that it'll persist. It'll make a difference. It will inspire all people yet to come." —Joel Cunningham

The Team of 1899 is part of the DNA of Sewanee. There are remembrances of the team all around campus: the stained-glass window in All Saints, Tremlett Springs still flowing, the dedication of the original gym in memory of Ormond Simkins, the plaque in Fowler Gym showing Henry G. Seibels as a college football All-American,[74] the spike over the football locker room that players tap as they exit for every game, and the plaque on the flagpole at the football field given by Ralph Black to honor his teammates.

"When I think about that band of brothers who fought side by side, first for each other, then for the honor of their school, it is evidence of our continued reverence for the display of character that made that team possible, and that is worth embracing forever." —Brigety

"Really, in athletics it is the ultimate David versus Goliath story." —Webb

"It seems like mythology. It just is such an amazing story that it's mythic; it's almost too fantastic to believe." —Brad Gioia

"Sewanee will be remembered as long as they're lacing up the football." —L. Majors

"That this little-known school could go on this barnstorming tour and come out on the other side victorious sets them apart from any other team that'll be fielded in the future history of college football. It's certainly the greatest—if not the single-most impressive—road trip a team has ever been on. It will never be topped." —Savage

"They were one of the first teams that actually traveled a long distance to play games. The fact that the greatest part of the achievement is surviving the brutality of it, ... the travel and the nature of the game itself." —Stephens

"I think all of us who enjoy the game now need to look back and sort of look at where the game started, how it evolved, and appreciate what the teams did within their timeframe. That's where Sewanee comes in. Within the context of its time, what the

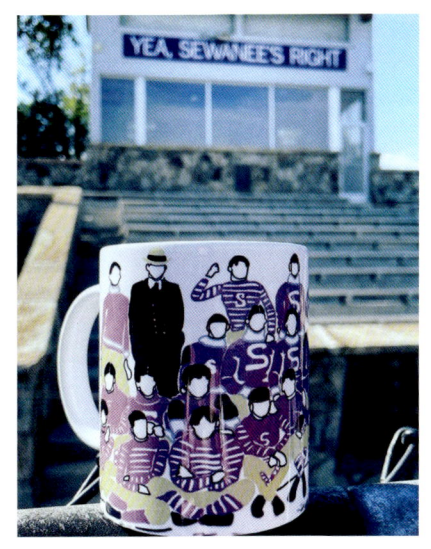

Left: Plaque on flagpole at Hardee-McGee Field commemorating the 1899 Team, donated by Ralph P. Black **Above:** 1899 mug designed by Sewanee graduate Casey George

"One of the many things that I have learned through my years involved with Sewanee Athletics is that, if nothing else, Sewanee is a place built on tradition. There are strengths in relying on that history. When the trail has already been traveled with honor, integrity, perseverance, and the many values we hope to uphold, then we raise the expectations of our own journey. The Iron Men of 1899 left that gift for generations that followed. Yet when we become too dependent on our past successes, we fail to raise the bar for those that follow us. Championship teams understand that. Undefeated seasons demand that. Just as the railroad journey found uncharted territory as it crossed state lines, our calling today is to seek out that adventurous spirit in today's pursuit of victory. The railroad remains a remarkable symbol of Sewanee's past, and a reminder of the journey ahead."

—John Shackelford

Above: Football locker room

Sewanee team of 1899 did is, to me, the greatest accomplishment of any college football team."
—Barnhart

Fuzzy Woodruff's words in his 1928 book, *A History of Southern Football, 1890-1928*, still resound today: "[I]n 1899 a new luminary flashed through the Southern firmament and its light remained shining, a story of the very first magnitude for many, many long years. That team was the Purple of The University of the South of Sewanee." [75]

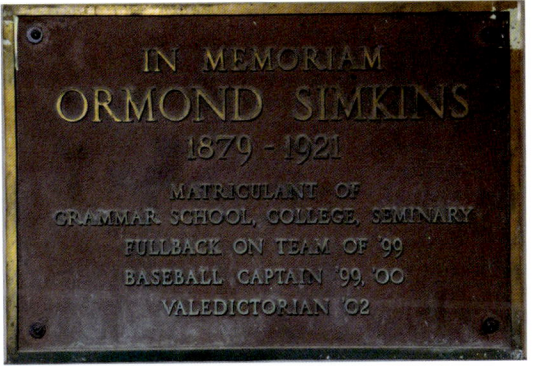

Left: Henry Seibels' Hall of Fame recognition
Above, top: Plaque honoring Ormond Simkins
Above, bottom: Tremlett Springs

"What they did is remarkable 125 years ago. It's going to be remarkable 125 years from now. It's going to be one of those things that absolutely people will look back and go, 'That's unbelievable.' But they did it."
—Barnhart

153 | 1899 REMEMBERED

The Miracle of Sewanee

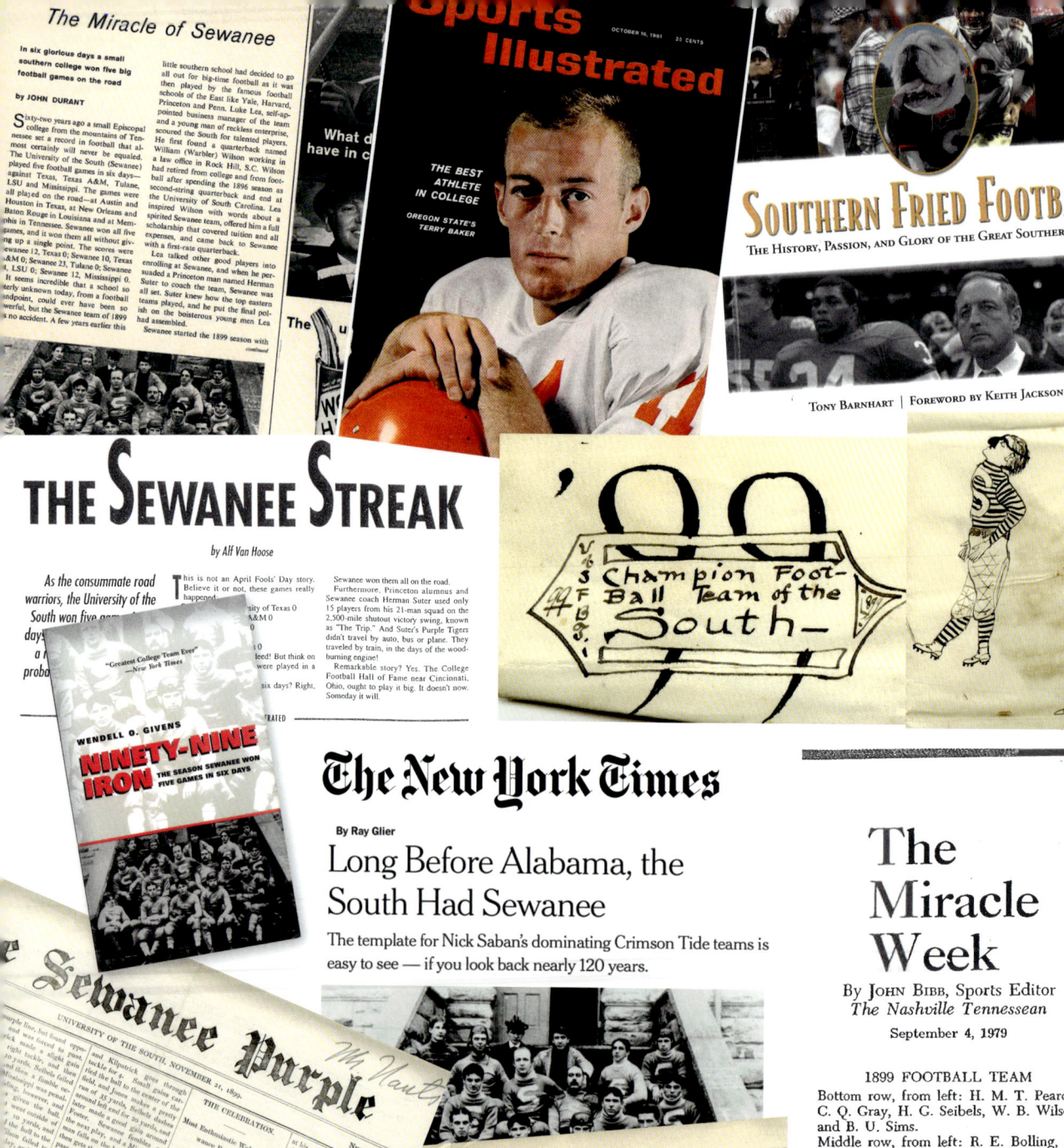

In six glorious days a small southern college won five big football games on the road

by JOHN DURANT

SOUTHERN FRIED FOOTBALL

THE HISTORY, PASSION, AND GLORY OF THE GREAT SOUTHERN GAME

TONY BARNHART | FOREWORD BY KEITH JACKSON

THE SEWANEE STREAK

by Alf Van Hoose

As the consummate road warriors, the University of the South won five games...

'99 Champion Football Team of the South

NINETY-NINE IRON
THE SEASON SEWANEE WON FIVE GAMES IN SIX DAYS
WENDELL O. GIVENS

"Greatest College Team Ever" — *New York Times*

The New York Times

By Ray Glier

Long Before Alabama, the South Had Sewanee

The template for Nick Saban's dominating Crimson Tide teams is easy to see — if you look back nearly 120 years.

The Miracle Week

By JOHN BIBB, Sports Editor
The Nashville Tennessean
September 4, 1979

1899 FOOTBALL TEAM
Bottom row, from left: H. M. T. Pearce, C. Q. Gray, H. G. Seibels, W. B. Wilson and B. U. Sims.
Middle row, from left: R. E. Bolling, R.

DEADSPIN

The Future Of College Football Is ... The University Of The South?

By Adam Doster
Published November 10, 2014

We may earn a commission from links on this page.

Larry Majors saunters toward Hardee-McGee Field—the oldest on-campus football stadium in the South—from the brick house his family has owned for nearly 50 years, the one so close that a rusty tackling dummy practically sits in the front yard. He passes a flagpole behind the east

CHAPTER 5

GREAT TEAMS

Southern Fried Football's All-Time Teams and...

THE TOP 25

1. Sewanee, 1899 (12–0)

The Tigers from Tennessee went 12–0 in 1899, but that's not why this team is number one. In November 1899 Sewanee took the ultimate road trip, playing five games in six days. Not only did the Tigers win them all, but all five wins were by shutouts. The Tigers began their trip at Texas (12–0) and then beat Texas A&M (10–0), Tulane (23–0), LSU (34–0), and Ole Miss (12–0) by a combined score of 91–0. Before the trip, Sewanee had beaten Georgia, Georgia Tech, and Tennessee. After the trip Sewanee closed out the season with a 71–0 win over Cumberland, an 11–10 win over Auburn (the o...

1899: A team representing the University of the South, which is located in Sewanee, Tennessee, pulled off one of the greatest feats in the history of college football. Beginning on November 9, 1899, Sewanee won five games in six days, all against national powers (Texas, Texas A&M, Tulane, LSU, and Mississippi), all on the road, and by a combined score of 91–0. Sewanee went on to finish 12–0 and was declared the Southern football champion.

On December 8 John Heisman left Auburn to become the head coach at Clemson.

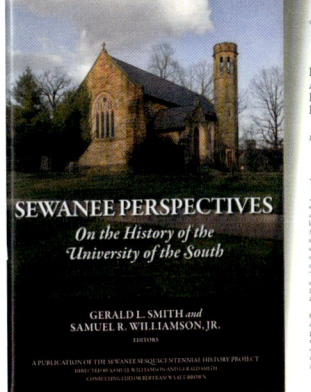

SEWANEE PERSPECTIVES
On the History of the University of the South

GERALD L. SMITH and SAMUEL R. WILLIAMSON, JR., Editors

A PUBLICATION OF THE SEWANEE SESQUICENTENNIAL HISTORY PROJECT

Remembering Ninety-Nine Iron: A Historical Perspective on the Legendary Football Team That Won Five Games in Six Days

Woody Register

In late August 1954 Sewanee's publicity director, Arthur Ben Chitty, wrote to an editor at *Sports Illustrated* to convince him to run a story on Sewanee's legendary football team of 1899. "For some time," Chitty asserted obliquely, he had been meaning to offer this "unfailable" story but a national magazine. "I believe you are the man who would be most interested in a story of this kind." Chitty's sense of timing and his estimation of the magazine were impeccable. *Sports Illustrated* was brand new; its first edition had come out only that month, the latest title in the Henry Luce Time-Life publishing empire. The new magazine sought outlets that transcended time and place, and that went beyond detailing the outcomes of contests, to capture the dramatic and universal essence of sport. What they needed, Chitty was certain, were stories like that of Sewanee's superhuman "Iron Men," who, over the course of six successive days in November 1899, traveled more than 2,500 miles and vanquished five foes: Texas, Texas A&M, Tulane, Louisiana State University (LSU), and Ole Miss, in the order He was right. *Sports Illustrated* promptly responded to say it was "interested."

Chitty's elation upon receiving his answer was palpable. Sewanee, which had floundered financially through the Depression years, and was growing impoverished along with the rest of higher education after the war, but the university still needed publicity and the legitimacy and advertising payoff conferred by national recognition. With *Sports Illustrated*, Chitty knew he had hit the big time with a story that was largely unknown outside the local confines of students and graduates. He immediately began ransacking the college's archives for materials and then launched a letter campaign to collect memories, anecdotes, and information from the few...

Scrapbook

A small sampling of accounts, old and new, about this amazing team and its season

---

Sewanee's iron men
BY WENDELL GIVENS
Photo by Bob Adams

BIRMINGHAM NEWS MAGAZINE, Sept. 13, 1959

RARE IS THE COACH in this football land who hasn't cautioned the faithful that his schedule this Fall is much too rugged to expect more than, say, a .500 finish.

And when the season's returns are in three months hence, a reminder of the iron-man schedule may ease the paying-off pain for never-learn old grads.

But for a couple of Birmingham business executives who keep tab of football fortunes, talk of too-tough schedules is not apt to make much headway.

H. G. Seibels, president of Jemison-Seibels, Inc., and Herbert E. Smith, board chairman of Vulcan Rivet and Bolt Corp., recall a season 60 years ago ...

SOUTHERN FOOTBALL teams were beginning to make themselves felt in the 1890s, although not for another decade or two would the rest of the country admit it.

The University of the South at Sewanee, Tenn., was rapidly becoming a Dixie power. Its best gate was Vanderbilt, but because of a rift over receipts the two did not book a game for 1899.

To compensate for the lost revenue, Manager Luke Lea beefed up the Sewanee schedule somewhat. Herman Suter of Princeton had just moved in as head coach and apparently had no stays in the making for 1899.

Sewanee opened with a 12-0 victory over Georgia in Atlanta on Oct. 21; stayed over a day, then whipped Georgia Tech, 32-0. Back at home, Suter's team put Tennessee to rout, 51-0, on Oct. 28 and five days later polished off Southwestern, 54-0.

Impressive but preliminary. On Nov. 8 a Sewanee squad of 21 entrained at the mountain home and headed West on what surely is the most astounding football expedition on record.

AFTER A DAY and night of riding the squad took a brief morning workout at a wayside station in Texas, then headed into Austin and defeated the University of Texas, 12-0.

To celebrate, the Sewanee men attended a dance that evening, then boarded a sleeper for Houston and a next-day engagement with Texas A&M. The Aggies went down, 10-0.

Horse then? Nope, back to the rails and next day in New Orleans Tulane was beaten, 23-0. Came now a break—the Sabbath—and the Sewanee squad went sightseeing. Next day, next stop: Baton Rouge, and Louisiana State, 34-0. The following day at Memphis, Ole Miss surrendered, 12-0.

Only then did Suter's raiders head back to the mountain, there to recover. Five major opponents, five victories in six days, on a 2000-mile trip!

At this point, it may be assumed, any number of demands for the floor are being made for vigorous rebuttal. Weak opponents, haphazard play, little physical wear, none of today's pressure. Some are valid points, but there's the other side: Equipment was inadequate, making play more dangerous; substitutes rarely were used; games consisted of two halves of 35 minutes each; travel accommodations usually were catch-as-catch could.

HOW WOULD the 1899 Sewanee outfit rate with today's precision T e a m s ? It wouldn't; neither would the so-called wonder teams of the 1930s—that's getting into relativity or something akin; a team must be rated against its contemporaries.

Antichronically, Sewanee finished out the '99 season pasting Cumberland, 71-0; nosing out Auburn, 11-10, in the only game in which the Tennesseans were scored on; then beating North Carolina, 5-0, for the championship of the South.

For the figure faddists, that comes to 12 victories, no defeats; 327 points to 10; and all wrapped up in a six-week season.

The afore-mentioned H. G. Seibels was Captain "Diddy" Seibels, right halfback on the Sewanee team and one of the top ball-carriers of the day. Herbert E. Smith of Birmingham was a reserve and was on the squad that made the five-games-in-six-days swing.

★ ★ ★

H. G. Seibels, captain of the famed 1899 Sewanee team, likes to reminisce

---

1899 Sewanee Football Roster

Ralph Peters Black — Sylvania, Ga.
Richard Elliott Bolling — Edina, Tenn.
Preston Smith Brooks — Sewanee, Tenn.
William Sterling Claiborne — Amherst Co., Va.
Harris Goodwin Cope — Savannah, Ga.
Albert T. Davidson — Augusta, Ga.
Andrew Cleveland Estes — Spartanburg, S.C.
Charles Quintard Gray — Ocala, Fla.
Daniel Baldwin Hull — Savannah, Ga.
John William Jones — Marshall, Texas
Henry Sheriden Keyes — Cambridge, Mass.
R.F. Rex Kilpatrick — Bridgeport, Ala.
Joseph Lee Kirby-Smith — Sewanee, Tenn.

Landon Randolph Mason — Marshall, Va.
Floy Hoffman Parker — Canton, Miss.
William Henry Poole — Glyndon, Md.
Henry G. "Diddy" Seibels — Montgomery, Ala.
Ormond Simkins
Bartlet et Ultimus S
Hugh M. T. "Bunny"
William B. "Warble"

Head Coach: H.M
Manager: Luke L.
Trainer: Cal Burr

The beginnings of th

Football spawned the NCAA. By the early 1900s, the game was nearly abolished across the nation. Due to its rugged nature, and an offensive scheme known as the flying wedge, injuries were numerous. Many schools dropped the sport as players were getting killed and protective equipment wasn't standard. In 1905, President Theodore Roosevelt, forever an advocate of physical fitness, summoned college athletics leaders to two White House meetings to encourage... Chancellor NYU convened tutions to in ing rules. A York, th Association was founded IAAUS in 1906, and in 1910, I...

Birmingham, Ala., Seacoast Publishing, 1992.

Grantland Rice Says:

A Record Trip — And...

It is highly probable that few football fans today recall the name Herman Suter, and the remarkable ... he coached just 5 years ago. I ran into Suter yesterday and w... ted it over. Herman Suter was the Princeton quarterback who ran 95 ...ards against Harvard back around 1895 or 1896. He was ... wiry fastness and still is on the small side, with a ... around 140 pounds, with a crown ... shock of long blond hair, at least ... it was blond in those days.

His story of the 1899 Sewanee foot... team is the most remarkable foot... bal epic in all football history.

"We had 105 students at Sewanee ... I mean that season," Suter said, "... wanee being a small but famous ... university hid away in the Tennessee mountains."

"My football squad consisted of ... eighteen men, from which only ... twelve or fourteen could go ... twelve of us covered 2,500 miles ..." ...hidden away from ... with fastness ... crowds. ... "We finally finished the season with twelve straight victories over the best teams in the South. We had to do all the traveling. We had to be the invaders. But we had ... major football assets, and there wasn't a man on the team who had been proselyted or paid for in any way.

"First, we had the finest football spirit I had ever shown. Can you imagine a small squad today playing twelve-man squads, in six days, and a ... of kicking when removed to rest, ... having had full stamina and ... Second, we had to take more ... rivals could...

CHAPTER VI
THE RISE OF SEWANEE

Purple's Tremendous 1899 Schedule—Different Scholastic Year—Months of Practice—Georgia Defeated—Eminent Georgia Players—Valley Tech Coach—Sewanee Wins Another — Davidson's Debut—Tennessee Downs Georgia—A Wierd Decision—Referee Leaves Game Flat—Rules Are Changed—Auburn De Facto Victor—Forney Yarbrough—Georgia's Hard Luck—The Great Auburn—Sewanee Battle—College Spirit Rampant—Purple Outplayed—Questionable Decisions—Simpkins' Fine Punting—Purple Despondent — Huguley's Great Run—The Referee Again Steps In—Auburn's Costly Fumble—Another Close Call—Sewanee's Great Stand—The Purple is Champion.

UP with the season of 1899, Virginia and N... Carolina took turns about...
ern football...

TIMEOUT

All Saints' Chapel

"I love All Saints' Chapel. It has become the center of our campus. We have the stained-glass windows all around the main part of the nave and the chancel that show biblical themes, that show elements in the life of the nation. We've got windows to Shakespeare, but we've also got windows of the 1899 football team. It's a way of saying that life at Sewanee is whole and it's of one piece. We've put those symbols, and we say, 'This is who we are.' That football team is part of who we are." —J. Smith

Above and right: All Saints' Chapel, Sewanee, Tennessee

TIMEOUT

SEWANEE FOOTBALL TODAY

The University of the South, based on its early football success, was a founding member of the Southeastern Conference in 1932.[76] Sewanee left the conference after the 1940 season and has continued playing football as a non-athletic scholarship school in Division III. Since 1899, Sewanee has had two other undefeated seasons—1958 and 1963—both under Coach Shirley Majors.

"Very few folks get to experience the ghost of the past, the oneness with something that's a whole lot more established, more important than you as an individual." —Robert Black

"The football field of The University of the South is such hallowed ground because it is the same place where the team of 1899 played and where subsequent teams have played as well. Summoning that spirit is a blessing as our teams enter the same contest of grit, of sweat, sometimes of blood as their predecessors who played ahead of them have done as well." —Brigety

Sewanee still plays football in Division III, which does not permit athletic scholarships. Students play for the love of the game.

"With small, little Sewanee on top of a remote mountain in southeast Tennessee playing Division III football non-scholarship, I think the story is even more worthwhile over time. … The fog rolls in and, if you're sitting in the stands, you can't see anything on the field. We'll punt the ball, and you can hear if it was blocked, but you can't see where it's going to land or who has it. … It is a throwback to yesteryear." —Webb

Above: Sewanee 27, Rhodes 14, 118th meeting, Homecoming, October 27, 2018 **Right, top to bottom:** 1890s football game at Hardee Field; Present-day Hardee-McGee Field

As a founding member of the SEC, Sewanee has the right to rejoin the conference. According to former Athletic Director Mark Webb, however, "It ain't gonna happen."

1899 REMEMBERED

OVERTIME

1899 Team Later in Life

Ralph P. Black
He went on to become an engineer for the Pennsylvania Railroad and to fight in World War I. Later, he taught civil engineering at Sewanee and Georgia Tech. He was known as "Rip" and "the Major." He provided the plaque honoring the 1899 team, which was placed on the flagpole at Hardee-McGee Field. Black died on January 18, 1960, at age 78.

Richard Elliott "Pap" Bolling
He became a surgeon. When he contracted tuberculosis, he and his family moved west. He died on July 13, 1915, in Pasadena, California, at age 39 and is buried in Edna, Texas.

Preston Brooks, III
He was the grandson of Congressman Preston Brooks of South Carolina, who attacked Massachusetts Senator Charles Sumner with a walking cane on May 22, 1856, on the floor of the U.S. Senate. Brooks was a lifelong resident of Sewanee and operated the family business known as the P.S. Brooks store. He died on February 3, 1950, at age 67 and is buried in the University Cemetery in Sewanee.

Cal Burrows
After 1899, we know nothing of him save one photograph in a student's scrapbook. His role as an integral part of Sewanee's season was recognized by the Sewanee Sports Hall of Fame, which named Burrows a Trailblazer in 2024. Truly, he was an unsung hero whose legacy endures today.

William "Wild Bill" Claiborne
He became an Episcopal priest and served as a Chaplain with the 17th Infantry, 42nd Division in World War I. He became an Archdeacon in Tennessee. He founded St. Andrews School for Mountain Boys, the DuBose Memorial Training School, Emerald Hodgson Hospital, and re-founded St. Mary's Industrial School for Girls. He also wrote two books. He was a trustee of The University of the South. Claiborne became known as "an apostle to the mountaineers." "*An Apostle to the Mountaineers*," The Literary Digest, (New York, Dec. 7, 1912), p. 1068. One description of his service in the ministry reads: "[E]leven years ago he went into the mountains of East Tennessee and rolled up his sleeves. They are still up. … His name is a household word in every cove." Claiborne died on January 7, 1933, at age 60, and is buried in the University Cemetery.

Harris G. Cope
He was the captain of the 1901 football team, Sewanee's Assistant Coach in 1904, and Head Coach from 1909 to 1916. Later, he coached and served as the athletic director at Howard College in Birmingham. He died on September 24, 1924, at age 44.

Albert T. Davidson
He was a businessman in Augusta, Georgia, and a member of the National Guard. He died on March 14, 1946, at age 66.

Andrew C. Evins
He was a shipping clerk in Columbia, South Carolina, and died on June 9, 1922, at age 41.

Charles Quintard "Quint" Gray
Gray graduated with a master's degree in 1900 and worked as an insurance broker in Dallas, Texas. He died on January 11, 1906, of typhoid-pneumonia at age 27.

Daniel B. Hull
He later worked for a fertilizer company, a milling company, and in real estate in Savannah, Georgia, and died on September 29, 1967, at age 85. He and Henry Seibels died on the same date as the final surviving members of the team.

John W. "Deacon" Jones
He became an Episcopal priest and served in Texas, California, Iowa, Illinois, and Kansas. He died by suicide on October 8, 1923, in Kansas City, Missouri, at age 47.

Henry Sheridan Keyes
He finished medical school at Sewanee, became a doctor, and practiced in California. He died on July 29, 1955, at age 90.

Ringland "Rex" Kilpatrick
He was a New York builder and real estate investor. He later reconnected with John Heisman at the New York Athletic Club. Kilpatrick died on November 4, 1955, at age 74. His grandson Ringland Rex Bray graduated from Sewanee in 1976.

Joseph Lee Kirby-Smith
He was the son of Confederate Civil War General Edmund Kirby-Smith and was named for Joseph Lee Kirby-Smith, who died fighting for the Union at the Battle of Corinth. He was the captain of

the 1903 Sewanee Team and graduated with an M.D. in 1906. Kirby-Smith served in World War I and was a dermatologist and pioneer in tropical medicine in Jacksonville, Florida. He died on November 5, 1939, at age 57.

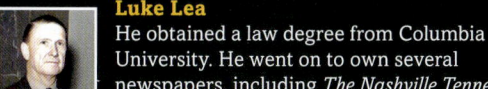

Luke Lea
He obtained a law degree from Columbia University. He went on to own several newspapers, including *The Nashville Tennessean* from 1907 to 1933. Lea hired his former coach, Billy Suter, to work for the newspaper. He became one of the youngest U.S. Senators ever when he was elected by the Tennessee legislature to the Senate in 1911 at age 32. Lea served in WWI and led a daring attempt to kidnap exiled German Kaiser Wilhelm II in Holland; they almost succeeded. He died on November 18, 1945, at age 66.

Landon R. Mason
He died of typhoid fever on April 13, 1902, shortly after graduating from Sewanee with a medical degree. He was about age 25.

Florence Hoffman "Floy" Parker
He was a prominent banker in Louisiana and Mississippi and died on April 18, 1954, at age 73.

Hugh Miller Thompson "Bunny" Pearce
His grandfather Hugh Miller Thompson, from England, was asked by Queen Victoria to preach her Jubilee sermon and later became the Bishop of Mississippi. Pearce became an Episcopal priest and served as a Chaplain in the U.S. Navy during World War I and for many years afterward. He died on November 24, 1935, at age 58.

William Henry Poole
After attending Sewanee as a theology student and football player, Poole finished his theology degree at the Episcopal Theological School in Cambridge, Massachusetts. He became an Episcopal priest and served in World War I as a Chaplain in France for the YMCA. He later worked as a priest in Michigan. Scarred by his war experiences, he took his own life with a gun on June 12, 1921, at age 45.

Henry G. "Ditty" Seibels
He became the headmaster of the Sewanee Grammar School after he graduated from Sewanee. He later worked as an insurance executive and founded Birmingham Fire Insurance Company and was later president of Jemison-Seibels. He was also an excellent golfer, winning the Alabama State Golf Championship in 1922. He was admitted into the College Football Hall of Fame in 1973, the Alabama Sports Hall of Fame in 1992, and the Sewanee Athletics Hall of Fame in 2004. Sewanee awarded him a Doctor of Civil Law degree in 1953. At his death on September 29, 1967, at age 91, Seibels was the oldest surviving member of the 1899 team. His teammate, Dan Hull, died on the same date at age 85.

Ormond Simkins
His father, William, allegedly loaded the cannon that fired the first shot of the Civil War at Fort Sumter. Simkins lived for many years in Corsicana, Texas, where he practiced law before going to work for the War Risk Bureau in Washington, D.C. He had to have one of his legs amputated due to injuries he had received while playing football. Unfortunately, he went back to have his second leg amputated at Georgetown Medical Hospital and died during that operation on December 4, 1921, at age 42.

Bartlett et Ultimas "The Caboose" Sims
Sims earned a medical degree from Tulane and served in the U.S. Army during World War I with the rank of captain. He later became a prominent physician and surgeon in Bryan, Texas. He died in a car wreck on January 5, 1934, at age 55.

Henry Milton "Billy" Suter
After coaching for several more years, he spent the bulk of his career in publishing, including working for the Nashville *Tennessean*, the *Washington Herald*, and the *Philadelphia Evening Star*. At the *Tennessean*, Suter gave famous sports writer Grantland Rice his first newspaper job. He died on October 31, 1946, at age 71.

William Blackburn "Warbler" Wilson
He became a member of the law firm of Wilson & Wilson and served as City Recorder (Municipal Judge) in Rock Hill, SC, for 35 years. In addition, he was elected to the South Carolina Legislature for two terms and served as Democratic State Committeeman from York County for three decades. Wilson died on December 8, 1958, at age 80. His great-great-granddaughter, Brucie Porter, graduated from Sewanee in 2020.

Left: Henry "Ditty" Seibels receiving honorary degree from Sewanee

THE PRESIDENT'S BOX

Above, left to right: Joel Cunningham, John McCardell, and Sam Williamson

"One hundred twenty-five years and more do not diminish the awesome legacy of the 1899 Sewanee football team. In three months (October to December) twelve victories included playing five in six days, and scoring a total of 322 points to 10 for their opponents with two classic victories over Auburn, 11-10, and the University of North Carolina, 5-0. All of this was done with twenty-one players at a time when players were not allowed to return to the game if they left. The result: Champions of the South.

Sewanee continued for another six years to play very competitive football, but after 1910 wins came more seldom and by 1920 even more so. Rule changes allowing substitutions, the introduction of the forward pass, and larger teams from larger student bodies that far outmeasured Sewanee, all contributed to the University moving in a different direction. By the mid-1930s Sewanee was no longer a competitive opponent. Entry into the new Southeastern Conference did not help since these teams could have scholarships and Sewanee did not. It never won a game in the conference. Its last SEC game was against Vanderbilt in 1940.

Still, the memories remain: brave men, relentless ambitions, adept playing and skillful use of the rules, and several players who obtained national recognition. It also helped that some of the victories were against teams that were just

162 | UNRIVALED: SEWANEE 1899

starting, and then the luck of playing Auburn and North Carolina last and in the Carolina case aided by darkness in Atlanta.

As Sewanee's football era slowly ended, there came a new status quo: pursuit of the Rhodes Scholarships. They would not replace football, but their presence gave Sewanee another pride that continues.

Sewanee has learned to adapt to change, keep its academic programs in place, and welcome new sports. Sewanee has adjusted to new summits, keeps pride in its memories, and has a clear relationship with reality."

—**Sam Williamson,** *14th Vice Chancellor*

"Colleges and universities are blessed if they have a distinctive saga, and The University of the South is especially blessed. Its saga is rooted in its splendid Mountain domain, its beautiful architecture, the deep affection and loyalty of its students and alumni, and Sewanee's glorious stories. Among its many great stories, that of the University's amazing 1899 football team holds a unique place. It will be a source of pride and joy for Sewanee folk for as long as we exist."

—**Joel Cunningham,** *15th Vice Chancellor*

"Though certainly an important chapter in the history of intercollegiate football, the story of the Sewanee 'Iron Men' of 1899 speaks across the years to us in our own time with a meaning that is in fact timeless. It is a story of commitment and courage, determination and stamina, selflessness and teamwork, sacrifice and loyalty. These values, exemplified during that extraordinary autumn, are worthy, indeed aspirational, in every season and generation and ought to be raised up as a clear representation of what it means to be marked forever as one of Sewanee's own. Yet we also are drawn to the preciously imperfect humanity of that roster and the reminder that all of us, now as well as then, must ever strive to seek a happy issue out of life's inevitable afflictions. May every member of the Sewanee family take this story and its lessons to heart, for it is not ancient history but, as the Greeks might have put it, 'philosophy teaching by example.' "

—**John McCardell,** *16th Vice Chancellor*

"Some lessons never grow old, including lessons about teamwork, determination, discipline and the confidence and hope of youth. Of course, examples of these lessons reinforce their ongoing meaning and significance. For us in the 21st century, there's no better example of these lessons than the story of the Sewanee football team at the close of the 19th century. And what a story it is!

Not just undefeated, going 12-0 in its 1899 season, but unscored upon except for Coach John Heisman's Auburn team, who managed 10 points against the Sewanee Tigers' 11 points, bringing the overall score of the season to Sewanee 322, opponents 10.

Not just games before a friendly home crowd at its Oxford-inspired campus on the Cumberland Plateau in Tennessee but games that took them, at one point in the season, on a grueling 2,500-mile railroad journey throughout the Deep South, including five games in a six-day stretch.

And, not just wins against similar small colleges with academics as the highest priority but victories over the likes of Texas, LSU, Ole Miss, North Carolina, and Georgia.

All possible because of teamwork, determination, discipline, and the confidence and hope of youth—lessons from the past, still important today, and vital for all generations to come."

—**Rob Pearigen,** *18th Vice Chancellor*

Above: Rob Pearigen

CHAPTER 12

The Documentary

"It's more than lore, it's true." —John McCardell

When my college classmate and friend Norman Jetmundsen first suggested that we collaborate on a film about Sewanee's famed 1899 football team, I figured the contours of the story would be largely lore with only fragments of truth. But as we dug deep into the story, we discovered a rich, dramatic, textured, and authentic story of grit, determination, ambition, skill, and perseverance. With the help of our generous donors, we were able to bring this compelling story to life on film.

In addition to telling a riveting and rare football story, our film explores the life, culture, and history of America in the late 1800s. Many of these men went on to serve in WWI and to have careers in business, law, politics, engineering, education, the ministry, and other fields of endeavor. Our film chronicles their successes and their many difficult challenges later in life.

This valuable book not only captures important archival material, but expands the orbit of *Unrivaled*, further preserving this remarkable and astonishing feat. **—David Crews**

Unrivaled: Sewanee 1899 was co-directed and co-produced by **David Crews** and **Norman Jetmundsen.** Major contributors to the film were: **Matthew Graves** (film editor); **Norman Jetmundsen** (script); **Ernie Eldridge** (fourteen original paintings); **Jim Trusilo** (two original paintings); **Bobby Horton** (music score); and **Gates Shaw** (main narrator). Many other people contributed in various ways to the film, all of whom are acknowledged in the credits.

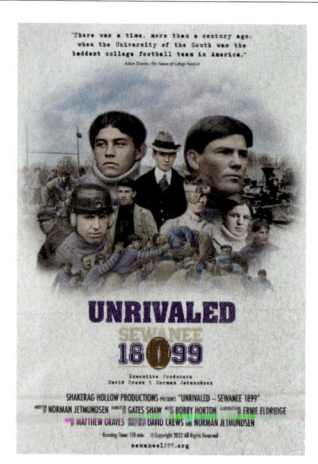

The film documents and dramatizes the amazing season of the 1899 Sewanee Tigers. More complete information is available on the website for the film and this book at: **sewanee1899.org.** The film is currently available for purchase via DVD or streaming, and it has been shown on most Public Television stations around the country, thanks to the sponsorship of Alabama Public Television. It has also been shown on Public Television's nationally distributed WORLD channel.

AWARDS AND ACCOLADES

Southeastern Regional Emmy
Nominated for Best Historical Documentary

Knoxville Film Festival
1st Place for Documentary Feature Film

Cobb International Film Festival
Best Local Film

Hollywood Gold Awards
Honorable Mention

164 | UNRIVALED: SEWANEE 1899

THE TEAM BEHIND *UNRIVALED*

David Crews

Lives in Oxford, Mississippi, Sewanee Class of '76. Executive Producer & Producer of *The Toughest Job*, which won a regional Emmy Award for Best Historical Documentary. Author of *The Mississippi Book of Quotations*. David named the film *Unrivaled*, and he has an uncanny ability to take the various threads of a film and weave them into a seamless story.

Matthew Graves

An Emmy Award-winning filmmaker based in Charleston, South Carolina, whose productions range from documentary and narrative films to commercial and promotional web videos. He received his bachelors degree in Broadcast Journalism from Hardin-Simmons University and a Masters of Arts in Language Education from the University of Mississippi. His colorization of the old photos brought them to life.

Bobby Horton

Bobby Horton is a Birmingham, Alabama, award-winning musician who is a multi-instrumentalist, composer, producer, and music historian. Horton has recorded Civil War songs of both the North and the South. He has provided music for a number of *Ken Burns* PBS documentaries, including the 1990 program on the Civil War. He has also contributed to the production of two programs for the *A&E Network*, and nine Civil War-related films for the *National Park Service*. He is a longtime member of the musical-comedy group *Three on a String* and has performed with the Front Porch String Band. His recordings of authentic period music have been internationally acclaimed.

Scan QR code to listen to Bobby Horton's music score from the documentary.
©Bobby Horton

Ernie Eldredge

Ernie Eldredge grew up in Homewood, Alabama, and art was always part of his life.

After obtaining a degree in Visual Design from Auburn University, he has spent his life as a designer, illustrator, and painter.

Eldredge's art is primarily representational, with a concentration on technique and a variety of visual styles. They are exercises that try to alter ordinary images, scenes, and figures into art that speaks to the individual.

His research and attention to detail for the illustrations in the film and in this book are likewise unrivaled.

Gates Shaw

A native of Birmingham, Gates attended Washington and Lee University and General Theological Seminary and was ordained as an Episcopal priest in 1981. He has served as a parish priest and with a wide range of ministries and non-profits seeking to help those in need.

He is known for his thought-provoking sermons and unselfish outreach to others.

He is also an avid outdoorsman.

Above, left to right: Battle Crews, Aubrey Black, and W. Marichal Gentry, re-enactors for the film.

"Certainly, the Sewanee team of '99 and what they did is unrivaled. It will never ever happen again. … No team ever in the history of college football will ever be able to do what they did."

—VINCE DOOLEY

AFTERWORD
by Norman Jetmundsen

"The story of '99 Iron lives not because of games and scores. It took Sewanee to a greater vision of itself. This is not just a story to brag about but a story to inspire. It became magical. It became something that not only inspired us about Sewanee football, it inspired the University to dream. Yea, Sewanee's Right!" —Jerry Smith

---

When my good friend and college classmate David Crews and I started talking about researching and producing a documentary film on the Sewanee Football Team of 1899, neither of us could have envisioned where the journey would lead. At the beginning, we both thought we would find a lot of lore about the team, but not much really factual. Were we ever wrong! As we dug into the research and interviewed historians, coaches, sports analysts, and descendants, we began to see that, in fact, in the words of the 16th Sewanee Vice Chancellor, John McCardell, "it's more than lore—it's true." I will not go into the making of the film, and the credits for that endeavor can be seen in the film. But suffice it to say the film allowed us the opportunity to dig deeply into this amazing team and its unbelievable season. It is indeed an "Unrivaled" team and a mythic story. We commend our documentary film to our readers.

We gathered so much rich material that I was compelled to do a book as well. This is a group effort with many people contributing to this project. The film and book would not have been possible but for the generosity of our donors. We also owe a great debt of gratitude to all the people who graciously allowed us to do interviews for the film. For this book, several people need special mention: first, David Crews, whose unwavering enthusiasm, hard work, and wise counsel made this endeavor possible; Matthew Graves, our video editor, who brought so much expertise to our film and story; our primary illustrator, Ernie Eldredge, who created many authentic re-creations of the season, along with several by Jim Trusilo; Woody Register and Matt Reynolds for their knowledge, research, and support; Buck Butler, who provided us with many beautiful photographs of Sewanee; Susan Alison and Taylor Jetmundsen for their meticulous and needed edits; Stephanie Gibson Lepore for footnote editing; Mary Lynn Porter, our executive assistant, whose tireless work made both the film and the book even possible; and Bobby Horton, Ann Jessup Gulledge, Susan Holmes, and Lane McGiboney for their assistance in adding the music to this book. Special acknowledgement and thanks goes to Karin Dupree Fecteau, whose patience and expertise in designing and formatting this book was amazing. Kelli Jetmundsen gave her characteristic and much needed love and support.

Additional research was conducted by Beth Hunter, Howard Jetmundsen, Taylor Jetmundsen, Cat Tumlin, and Katie Windle. Thank you to Robbey Stanford for exquisite printing. Finally, this film and book are a product of the education David and I received at The University of the South. Sewanee gave us lifelong friendships, a broad liberal arts education, amazing professors, and a solid foundation to live rich and productive lives. We first bonded during an assignment for Dr. John Reishman on Tennyson's *Ulysses*, which is still one of my favorite poems.

> **"I am a part of all that I have met;**
> **Yet all experience is an arch wherethro'**
> **Gleams that untravell'd world,**
> **whose margin fades**
> **For ever and for ever when I move."**

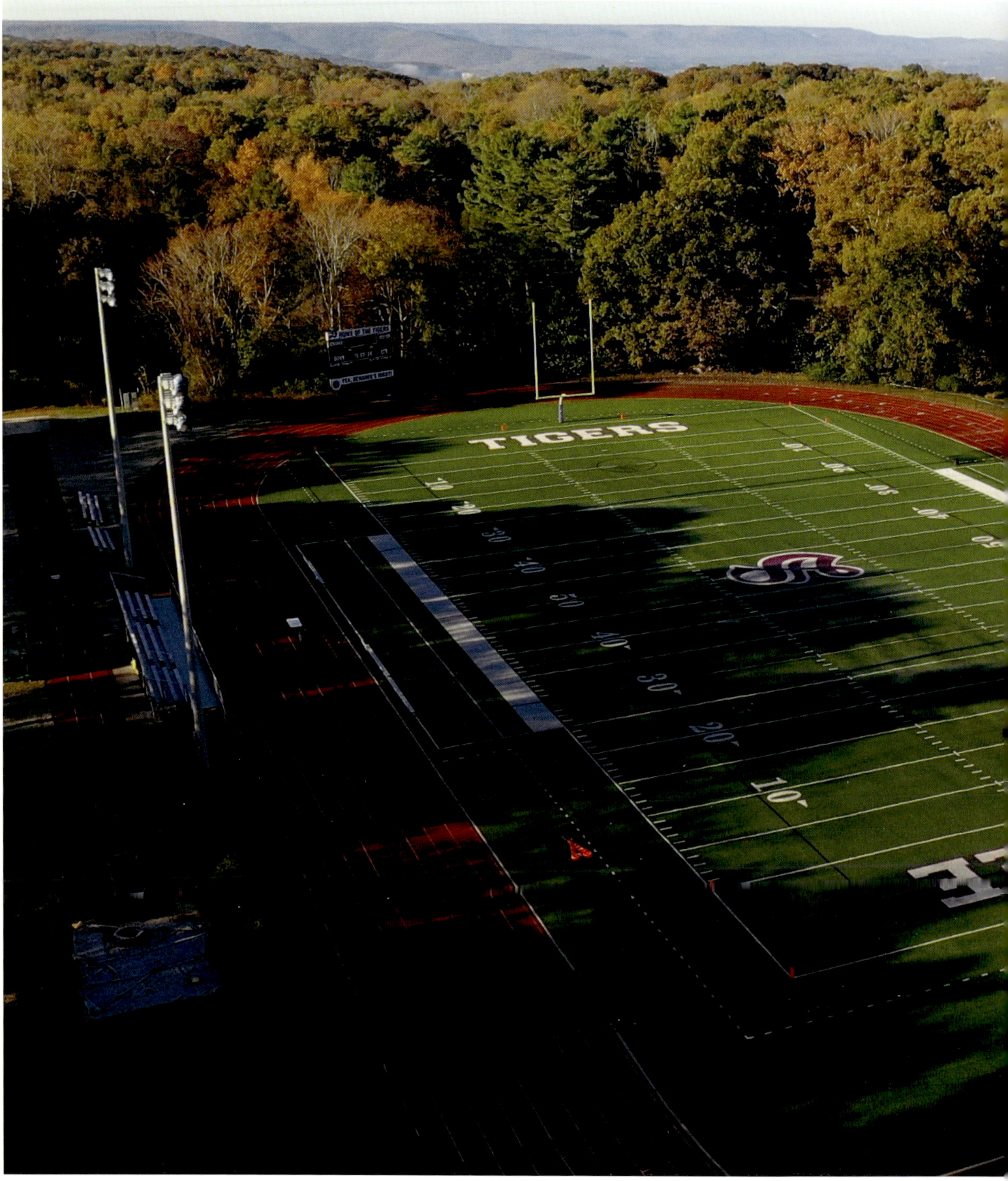
TIGERS

"Originally Hardee Field, it became McGee Field and then became historic Hardee-McGee Field. It is the oldest field in the South. It's the fourth oldest in the country, and we've been playing football on it since 1891." —Mark Webb

FOOTNOTES

1. Adam Doster, "The Future of College Football Is…The University of the South?", DEADSPIN, November 10, 2014, deadspin.com.

2. Wayne Hester, *Where Tradition Began: The Centennial History of Auburn Football* (Birmingham, AL: Seacoast Publishing, 1991).

3. Ed Miles, "7-Day, 5-Game Grid Trip Recalled by Tech Prof," *The Atlanta Constitution,* November 23, 1944.

4. The note under this illustration reads: "Enthusiasts for Rugby football in this country would scarcely recognise the game as it is played on the other side of the Atlantic. There, the game must, indeed, be rough, to judge by the costume assumed by the players, who not only wear shin protectors, padded clothes, ear protectors, but even nose protectors, which give them a singularly dissipated and ruffianly aspect."

5. Ed Miles, "Sub Rule Makes for Sissies, 1899 Sewanee End Declares," *The Atlanta Journal,* February 5, 1950.

6. "'Nearly every death may be traced to "unnecessary roughness." Picked up unconscious from beneath a mass of other players, it was generally found that the victim had been kicked in the head or stomach, so as to cause internal injuries or concussion of the brain, which, sooner or later, ended life,' *The Post* wrote on October 15, 1905." Katie Zezima, as excerpted in "How Teddy Roosevelt Helped Save Football," *The Washington Post,* May 29, 2014.

7. Brian Meehl, "Dateline 1905: Why Did Teddy Roosevelt Want Football to be Banned?", *BookTrib,* October 19, 2016.

8. Herbert E. Smith, letter to Arthur B. Chitty, October 12, 1954.

9. Ed Miles, "Sub Rule Makes for Sissies, 1899 Sewanee End Declares," *The Atlanta Journal,* February 5, 1950.

10. Wayne Hester, *Where Tradition Began: The Centennial History of Auburn Football* (Birmingham, AL: Seacoast Publishing, 1991). Dr. Thomas B. Quigley, an esteemed team physician for Harvard athletics, once said, "Whenever young men gather regularly on green autumn fields, or winter ice, or polished wooden floors to dispute the physical possession and position of various leather and rubber objects according to certain rules, sooner or later somebody is going to get hurt."

11. Herbert E. Smith, handwritten notes to Arthur B. Chitty, October 1954.

12. Southern Intercollegiate Athletic Association, 1895 Constitution, Article II (Athens, GA), 1895. *The Sewanee Purple* listed as one of the rules for the Southern Intercollegiate Athletic Association in 1898: "Any member of a team using profane or vulgar expressions on the field in any contest shall be disqualified by the umpire for the remainder of the contest." *The Sewanee Purple,* May 14, 1898.

13. Caspar W. Whitney, "Amateur Sport," *Harper's Weekly,* January 7, 1899.

14. Sewanee alumnus Jack Blackwell, who graduated in 1947 after serving in the Pacific for the Navy in WWII and who passed away in 2024 at 103 years old, recounted this Sewanee cheer from his student days: "Sewanee was Sewanee, when Vandy was a pup, Sewanee'll be Sewanee when Vandy's busted up. To hell, to hell with Vandy, and all its sorry crew, and if you went to Vanderbilt, to hell to hell with you!"

15. Herbert E. Smith, letter to Arthur B. Chitty, October 12, 1954.

16. Herbert E. Smith, handwritten notes to Arthur B. Chitty, undated.

17. Sewanee's 1899 Football Team, Seibels family files.

18. Arthur B. Chitty, letter to Gioia Grimes, November 5, 1954.

19. G. Rice, "Grantland Rice Says: A Record Trip and a Record Team," *The News* (Paterson, NJ), November 22, 1944.

20. James N. Young, letter to Ralph P. Black, October 25, 1954.

21. Seibels' nickname has been spelled both "Ditty" and "Diddy." Because early correspondence between members of the team and Seibels, as well as several articles written while he was alive use "Ditty," we chose that spelling.

22. G. Rice, "Grantland Rice Says: A Record Trip and a Record Team," *The News* (Paterson, NJ), November 22, 1944.

23. Sewanee's 1899 Football Team, Seibels family files.

24. G. Rice, "Grantland Rice Says: A Record Trip and a Record Team," *The News* (Paterson, NJ), November 22, 1944.

25. Herman Helms, "Herman Helms' Sports Shots," *The Charlotte Observer,* July 30, 1953.

26. Herbert E. Smith, letter to Arthur B. Chitty, December 6, 1948.

27. Arthur B. Chitty, letter to Gioia Grimes, October 21, 1954.

28. Sewanee's 1899 Football Team, Seibels family files.

29. Sewanee's 1899 Football Team, Seibels family files.

30. Grantland Rice, "That Record Team Recalled," *The News* (Paterson, NJ), November 22, 1944.

31. James N. Young, letter to Ralph P. Black, December 2, 1954.

32. William B. Wilson, letter to Arthur B. Chitty, October 18, 1954.

33. Jerry Bryan, "Five Games in Six Days Was Record of Sewanee Eleven Under Seibels," May 29, 1932, Seibels family files.

34. "The Sewanee men…look to be trained in the most perfect style, having a healthy, peculiarly fresh look that is to be seen on the faces of all well-trained athletes. They appear not to weigh nearly as much as do the Georgia men, but they had an elastic step, and a healthy glow upon their cheeks. None seemed to be the least overstrained, and all appeared to be finished in a fine style…. All of the Sewanee men are old, experienced players, and know the game in all its intricate points." *The Atlanta Constitution,* October 21, 1899.

35. Herbert E. Smith, handwritten notes to Arthur B. Chitty, October 1954.

36. The Sewanee Athletic Souvenir, The University of the South, 1901.

37. William B. Wilson, letter to Arthur B. Chitty, October 18, 1954.

38. *The Sewanee Purple,* October 31, 1899, Arthur B. Chitty reported Dan Hull said, "On the trip to Texas I do not remember any complaints about the schedule being too tough. All the boys seemed to feel it was a great lark and lots of fun." Arthur B. Chitty, letter to Gioia Grimes, November 5, 1954.

39. *The Sewanee Purple,* December 14, 1899.

40. Arthur B. Chitty, letter to H. Helfer, December 10, 1948.

41. *The Sewanee Purple,* November 14, 1899.

42. Official Record of Team, Seibels family files.

43. "Sewanee 12, Varsity 0," *Daily Statesman,* November 10, 1899.

44. *The Sewanee Purple,* Football Number, December 14, 1899.

45. Ralph P. Black, letter to Henry G. Seibels, August 25, 1949.

46. *Bryan Morning Eagle,* November 12, 1899.

47. Luke Lea, telegram to Benjamin L. Wiggins, November 11, 1899.

48. The Olive and Blue, Tulane University, November 16, 1899.

49. *The Sewanee Purple,* December 14, 1899.

50. "Sewanee Continues on Her Triumphal March Through the Southern States," *The Reveille,* November 15, 1899.

51. Rufus Ward, "Ask Rufus: The greatest football team ever," *The Dispatch,* February 5, 2012, cdispatch.com/lifestyles/article.asp?aid+15490.

52. "The Fifth Shut-Out," *The Commercial Appeal,* November 15, 1899.

53. Benjamin L. Wiggins, letter to Silas McBee, November 28, 1899.

54. Henry G. Seibels, letter to Luke Lea, March 12, 1943.

55. Ed Miles, "7-Day, 5-Game Grid Trip Recalled by Tech Prof," *The Atlanta Constitution,* November 23, 1944.

56. Luke Lea, letter to Henry G. Seibels, April 7, 1943.

57. William B. Wilson, letter to Arthur B. Chitty, October 18, 1954.

58. Luke Lea, letter to Henry G. Seibels, April 7, 1943.

59. Squire Brown, "Sporting News," *Montgomery Advertiser,* December 13, 1899.

60. "Coach Heisman Scores Officials," *The Age-Herald,* December 4, 1899.

61. "Umpire Taylor Answers Heisman," *The Age-Herald,* December 6, 1899.

62. Arthur B. Chitty, letter to M. Miller, November 27, 1954.

63. *The Evening Star,* Washington, D.C., December 5, 1935.

64. Ralph P. Black, letter to Henry G. Seibels, August 25, 1949.

65. *Cap and Gown,* The University of the South, 1900.

66. William B. Wilson, letter to Arthur B. Chitty, October 18, 1954.

67. *The Sewanee Purple,* Football Number, December 14, 1899.

68. *Cap and Gown,* The University of the South, 1900.

69. G. Rice, "Grantland Rice Says: A Record Trip and a Record Team," *The News* (Paterson, NJ), November 22, 1944.

70. Wendell O. Givens, *Ninety-Nine Iron: The Season Sewanee Won Five Games in Six Days* (Tuscaloosa, AL: The University of Alabama Press, 2003).

71. A book titled *Yale's Ironmen* by William N. Wallace, about the Yale team of 1934, calls them the Ironmen because all eleven players played one entire game against Princeton. With all due respect to our Bulldog friends, we believe Sewanee's 1899 team are the true Iron Men.

72. Ormond Simkins, letter to William Claiborne, May 2, 1916.

73. James N. Young, letter to Ralph P. Black, October 25, 1954.

74. In an August 22, 1949, letter, Seibels wrote to Ralph Black, his former roommate, "I have dictated the story [of the 1899 team] but it sounds pretty sorry to me. As a matter of fact, I can't see how anybody would be interested in knowing about a football team that played fi y years ago." Henry G. Seibels, letter to Ralph P. Black, August 22, 1949. Several days later, he added: "The story of the 1899 Team is interesting to a few of the old-timers and especially to those who participated and are still living, but I cannot see that there is any excuse for publishing it in *Goodhousekeeping* [sic] or any other magazine." Henry G. Seibels, letter to Ralph P. Black, August 26, 1949.

75. Fuzzy Woodruff, *The Rise of Sewanee, A History of Southern Football 1890-1928, Vol. 1* (Atlanta, GA: Georgia Southern Publishing Co., 1928).

76. Sewanee was such a fierce early rival of the University of Alabama that Alabama's original "Yea Alabama" fight song, composed in 1926, had this opening stanza: "Let the Sewanee Tiger scratch, Let the Yellow Jacket sting, Let the Georgia Bulldog bite, Alabama still is right!"

PHOTO AND ARCHIVAL SOURCES

Special note: Many of the original black-and-white photos have been color-enhanced by Matthew Graves.

William R. Laurie University Archives and Special Collections for The University of the South: 4, 26-27, 29, 30-43, 45-48, 53-54, 56-58, 62-63, 66-67, 72, 76-77, 81, 84-85, 90, 95-97, 105, 115, 120-121, 126-127, 131, 134-135, 139-141, 159, 161
Footnotes: 8, 11, 12, 15, 16, 18, 20, 26, 27, 31, 32, 35, 36, 37, 38, 39, 40, 41, 44, 45, 47, 49, 54, 57, 58, 62, 65, 66, 67, 68, 72, 73, 74

Courtesy of The University of the South:
2, 142-153, 156-159, 162-163, 168-169

Library of Congress: 8, 16-17, 51

Scott Rogers: 10-11

Whitney, Caspar W., "The Nearest to Mass Formation Allowed by the New Rules," *Harper's Weekly*, Vol. XL, No. 2084, Harper & Bros., New York (November 28, 1896): 16

Carlisle Indians vs. Yale at the Polo Grounds in Bronx, NY, 1907. Here's the true story of how Teddy Roosevelt saved football: deseret.com/sports/2023/8/8/23819981/how-teddy-roosevelt-saved-football/ (December 25, 2023): 16

Whitney, Caspar W., "The Harvard-Yale Game-the Tandem Tackles-back, the Play that Won the Championship for Harvard," *Harper's Weekly*, Vol. 45, p. 1218, Harper's Magazine Company, New York (December 7, 1901): 17

College Football Hall of Fame, Atlanta, GA: 22-25

The University of Tennessee Betsey B. Creekmore Special Collections and University Archives: 28, 72

Vanderbilt University Athletic Department: 49

General Douglas MacArthur, Fighter for Freedom, Francis Trevelyan Miller, The John C. Winston Co., Chicago, IL, January 1, 1942, courtesy of the Bolling family: 56

"Football practice, showing players pushing a wooden tackling dummy," Looking Back at Tennessee Collection (7610), Tennessee State Library and Archives: 65

Hargrett Rare Book and Manuscript Library, University of Georgia Libraries: 66

gahistoricnewspapers.galileo.usg.edu/lccn/gua1179162/1899-11-04/ed-1/seq-1/: 66

"Georgia Tech Football Team of 1899," George C. Griffin Photograph Collection (VAC002_115), Archives and Special Collections, Crosland Library, Georgia Institute of Technology: 70

Rhodes College Archives Digital Repository: 75

PICA08144, Austin History Center, Austin Public Library: 84

PICA19721, Austin History Center, Austin Public Library: 86-87

Fisher, Larry Jene. [Photograph of 1900 Texas A&M Football Team], photograph, 1900; (texashistory.unt.edu/ark:/67531/metapth587378/), University of North Texas Libraries, The Portal to Texas History, texashistory.unt.edu; crediting Lamar University: 90

Image 976-1-4, Tulane University Howard-Tilton Memorial Library Special Collections: 94-95

en.wikipedia.org/wiki/1899_LSU_Tigers_football_team: 102

University of Mississippi Athletics Department Archives: 104

en.wikipedia.org/wiki/1903_Cumberland_Bulldogs_football_team: 114

University of North Carolina Libraries Southern Historical Collection: 115, 126

thewareaglereader.com/2011/12/john-heismans-letter-to-auburn-students-1899/: 116

1900 *The Glomerata:* Vol. 4, Auburn University Libraries Special Collections and Archives: 116

Seibels family 1899 Team files: 136-137

Ernie McCoy: 146

ORIGINAL ARTWORK

Ernie Eldridge: Pages 44, 60-61, 68-69, 72-73, 88-89, 92-93, 98-99, 101, 102-103, 106-107, 110-111, 118-119, 122-123, 124, 128-129, 132-133, 138

Jim Trusilo: Pages 74-75, 80

INTERVIEWS FOR FILM QUOTED IN THIS BOOK

Interviews with the following people were conducted in 2017-2021 and are excerpted herein.

Yogi Anderson, former Sewanee player, assistant coach and alumni director

Tony Barnhart, author and CBS Sports commentator

Ralph Black III, Ralph P. Black's grandson

Robert Black, former Sewanee player and head coach and current development officer

Bobby Bowden, former head football coach at Florida State University

Rex Bray, Ringland "Rex" Kilpatrick's grandson

Reuben Brigety, 17th Vice Chancellor at The University of the South

Joel Cunningham, 15th Vice Chancellor at The University of the South

Vince Dooley, former head football coach and athletic director at the University of Georgia

Fred Faircloth, William "Warbler" Wilson's great-grandson

Brad Gioia, former head of school at Montgomery Bell Academy

Kirk Herbstreit, commentator for ESPN and Gameday

Kevin Jones, former Sewanee player

Laura Knox, Luke Lea's daughter

Johnny Majors, former head football coach at the University of Tennessee and University of Pittsburgh

Larry Majors, former Sewanee player and assistant football coach

John McCardell, 16th Vice Chancellor at The University of the South

Jon Meacham, author and historian

Robert Miller, sports orthopedic surgeon

John Morrow, attorney

Wyatt Prunty, editor, poet, and author

Woody Register, history professor at The University of the South

Leah Rubino, Luke Lea's granddaughter

Travis Rundle, former Sewanee head football coach

Nick Saban, former head football coach at the University of Alabama

174 | UNRIVALED: SEWANEE 1899

Phil Savage, former Sewanee football player and current sports analyst and NFL scout

Frances Seibels, Henry "Ditty" Seibels' daughter-in-law

Henry Seibels III, Henry "Ditty" Seibels' grandson

Kelly Seibels, Henry "Ditty" Seibels' grandson

John Shackelford, athletic director at The University of the South

Jerry Smith, former religion professor at The University of the South

Ken Smith, forestry professor at The University of the South

Kent Stephens, former curator at the College Football Hall of Fame and historian

Crom Tidwell, Luke Lea's grandson

Mark Webb, former athletic director at The University of the South

Sam Williamson, 14th Vice Chancellor at The University of the South

Above: THE QUAD AT SEWANEE, by Bob Askew

ABOUT THE AUTHOR
Norman Jetmundsen, Jr.
Retired attorney in Birmingham, Alabama, and former Trustee of The University of the South. He is a graduate of Sewanee, Class of '76, The University of Alabama Law School, and Oxford University (Magdalen College). In addition to his work on the film, he is the author of two other novels and several published essays.

ABOUT THE CO-AUTHOR
Karin Dupree Fecteau
International award-winning Alabama-based graphic designer specializing in publications, brand development, advertising, nonprofit design work, and digital experience. She worked as a Senior Designer for *Southern Living* magazine before starting her own design studio in 2012. She is a graduate of Auburn University, Class of '93.

This book, **Unrivaled: Sewanee 1899**, is available at: **sewanee1899.org**.
Thanks to Derick Belden and FRED for their professional design of the website.
The documentary film is available on DVD or streaming formats.
For questions about the book or film, please contact us at: **sewanee1899@gmail.com**.
You can find up-to-date information about the book and film on
Facebook **(Unrivaled)** or Instagram **(@sewanee1899)**, as well as our website.
For information about **The University of the South**, please visit: **sewanee.edu**.